Amazing Stories
to Tell and Retell ▪ 1

Amazing Stories to Tell and Retell ■ 1

Lynda Berish
Marie-Victorin College

Sandra Thibaudeau
Marie-Victorin College

Houghton Mifflin Company
Boston ■ New York

Director of ESL Programs: *Susan Maguire*
Senior Associate Editor: *Kathleen Sands Boehmer*
Developmental Editor: *John Chapman*
Editorial Assistant: *Kevin Evans*
Project Editor: *Anne Holm*
Senior Manufacturing Coordinator: *Priscilla J. Abreu*
Marketing Manager: *Patricia Fossi*

Cover design: Harold Burch Design, NYC

Photo credits: p. 2, AP/Wide World Photos; p. 16, Allen McInnis/
Montreal Gazette; p. 21, David Barclay Rossiter; p. 29, Calgary Sun;
p. 42, John Kenney/Montreal Gazette; p. 59, Danny Greyson; p. 100,
Montreal Gazette; p. 105, Phil Norton/Montreal Gazette

ACKNOWLEDGMENTS

"Money from the Sky." Adapted from "Pennies from Heaven . . . and
Quarters and Bills, Too" from the *Los Angeles Times*. "Save My Mom!"
Used by permission of Joanne Brissette. "My Brother's in the Dryer!"
Used by permission of Kim Tarbell. "Couriers in the Cold." Used by
permission of Jeff Chiperzak and Shaun Finnis. "The Biggest Pumpkin."

Acknowledgments continue on page 143, which constitutes an extension
of the copyright page.

Printed in the U.S.A.

Library of Congress Catalog Card Number: 98-71985

ISBN: 0-395-88440-3

4 5 6 7 8 9—SB—02 01 00

Contents

www.hmco.com/college

Introduction

Amazing Stories to Tell and Retell 1 is an adult reader for students at the high beginning and intermediate language levels. The book is designed to get students reading—and talking! The unusual topics of these human-interest stories capture students' attention and make them want to find out more. The language in the stories has been carefully controlled to allow high beginners to understand the ideas and to enable them to use the stories to improve their reading skills and expand their vocabularies.

Amazing Stories consists of ten units, each of which contains a pair of thematically linked stories. All units follow an identical format. A series of activities before each story is used to pique students' interest and to build background for the reading passage. Follow-up activities after each story help students better understand what they have read and also provide opportunities for vocabulary expansion. The unit wrap-up, called Put It Together, presents a language review and helps students make connections between the stories and the outside world. A key feature of the Put It Together section is the Tell the Stories activity, which guides students as they tell the stories in their own words, first to another student and then to someone outside the class.

THE STORIES

Every story in *Amazing Stories* is true. Over the years, we found these unusual anecdotes in magazines and newspapers and used them to motivate our students to read and to discuss what they had read. As we put the book together, we contacted and interviewed as many of the people in the stories as possible to check that the information was accurate and to discover other aspects of the tales that would add spice to these already remarkable stories. We would like to offer our heartfelt thanks to all the people who shared their stories. They were all extremely helpful, and their willingness to have their experiences included in this book will mean a lot to all the students who use it.

THE UNIT FORMAT

Each unit follows a set format.

- The unit opens with a Let's Get Ready page that stimulates students' interest and gets them involved in the unit. One aim of this section is to explore students' prior knowledge of the topic. New vocabulary is introduced, and students are often asked to make predictions about the readings that follow.

- Immediately preceding the opening of each story is a Before You Read section, which contains vocabulary work, categorizing activities, and questions relating to the pictures that accompany the story.

- The Reading Skills section that follows each story comprises many different types of activities. The most commonly used tasks involve general reading comprehension and vocabulary building and reviewing. However, several other types of exercises are featured. Among them are Scan for the Details, Review the Pronouns, Understand the Details, Give Your Opinion, and Explain Why. Some of these activities incorporate productive language responses in addition to receptive reading skills.

- The Put It Together section at the end of each unit contains several summary activities covering both stories. Let's Review provides a review of the events and vocabulary in the two stories. Tell the Stories helps students integrate the new language by telling the stories in their own words. They are given a variety of prompts and suggestions to make this process fun and interesting. Talk About It and Solve the Problem provide useful suggestions for group work.

- Two other features appear in many Put It Together sections. In Your Neighborhood contains activities that help students make connections between the stories and their own communities. Writing Option suggests ideas for written follow-ups related to the unit topic.

TELL AND RETELL

One key feature of this book is the way it enables and encourages students to tell and retell the stories. This activity stems from the desire most of us have to share unusual or interesting stories we hear. Students are led through a series of steps that help provide the understanding of the story and the language practice they need to feel confident telling the story.

- First they read the stories and do the reading and language exercises that accompany them.

- Next they each tell the story to a peer in class. This provides an opportunity for sheltered practice.

- Then the student is invited to tell the story to an English speaker outside of class.

These retellings serve two purposes. First, as students talk about what they have read, they integrate the new language and make it their own. Second, the out-of-class retellings provide students who are embarrassed to speak English or who feel they have nothing interesting to say in English an opportunity to feel proud of their ability to tell a strange or funny story. After practicing the story, students leave the classroom speaking English.

SOME TIPS ON TELLING AND RETELLING

The stories in this book can be used in many different ways. The activities outlined provide a basic framework. The teacher can then build on this framework to meet the needs of students of different ages, interests, and cultural backgrounds.

- In multilevel classes, teachers may wish to assign the second story in the unit (which is slightly more difficult than the first) to the more able readers. Or teachers may wish to survey the stories with the class and then allow students to select the one they think is best for them.

- Teachers may assign partners to work on a story together. When they are ready to tell the story to each other, they will be able to help each other remember details and vocabulary and formulate the sentences they need. Contrary to what we may think, students do not get bored telling the same story more than once. They appreciate the chance to practice their new language and build confidence in speaking English.

- Another classroom activity can involve having each student tell the story to another student who did not read it. During this phase, teachers should encourage the listener to be an *active* listener, asking questions and discussing the story afterward.

- Another option is to have students tell the story they heard, not the one they read. This encourages active listening and provides additional oral practice.

- Here are some other possibilities.
  1. Have students record the stories on tape and listen to themselves speak.
  2. Ask students to tell the story to the teacher first and then to another student.
  3. Suggest that students write out the story in their own words before they tell it.

- After the classwork is finished, the final step is for students to tell the story to someone outside the class. If students have difficulty finding an English speaker to converse with, teachers can help them find ways to structure this activity.
  1. Have students visit another classroom and tell the stories to students there.

2. Arrange lunchtime or after-school activities where English speakers will be present.
3. Have students visit a community center or senior center where they will have a chance to practice speaking English and telling the stories.

RATIONALE

The approach used in *Amazing Stories* is from the communicative model of language learning. It teaches reading strategies through a variety of interactive activities. Students work with partners to reinforce language and to help the other person learn. The dynamic classroom atmosphere that this creates draws students into focusing on content rather than on discrete aspects of language.

Reading skills are supported through a careful progression of activities. Pre-reading activities help students get started. Thematic units help students focus on content. The telling and retelling component gives students a real purpose for reading since they have a specific goal—to tell the story to someone else when they are through. This helps them to read with more interest and to remember more of what they read.

Amazing Stories features accessible vocabulary and simple sentence structures. Fundamental reading strategies, such as skimming to find the main idea and scanning for details, are introduced. The methodology aims to develop students' confidence as readers and to build vocabulary in a supportive environment with the help of interesting exercises and illustrations.

ACKNOWLEDGMENTS

We wish to thank:
- Kathy Sands Boehmer, who encouraged us through the writing stages and gave us valuable feedback about the stories
- Susan Maguire, who suggested these books and inspired us to write them
- Lauren Wilson, who found people and places for us and helped us with permissions
- John Chapman, whose enthusiasm and skillful editing helped shape the final product
- Allen Dykler, who gave us support and encouragement

We gratefully acknowledge our reviewers for their valuable input and suggestions. Thanks go to the following people:

Janet L. Eveler, El Paso Community College, Texas
Grazyna Kenda, State University of New York, Brooklyn, New York

Robin Longshaw

Denise Selleck, City College of San Francisco, California

Special thanks also go to:

- Our loving families, whose patience allowed us to spend many hours at our computers: Johnny, Tara, and Andrea Berish; Charles Gruss, Jean-Baptiste, Gaby, Annabel, Shem, and baby Tasnim
- Millicent and Max Goldman for providing us with a constant supply of newspapers and magazines, where we found many of the stories

We also gratefully acknowledge the following people, for giving us permission to tell their stories:

- Johanne and Chloé Brissette
- Kim, Robin, Dustin, and David Tarbell
- Jeff Chiperzak and Shaun Finnis
- Howard Dill
- Sandro Ravazzano
- Loretta Keith
- Pallas Hansen and Char Krumwiede
- Ryan Ruby, Mr. and Mrs. Ruby
- Mary and Lorne VanSinclair
- Jill, Jena, Doug, and Phil Malm
- Jenny Woznuk and Philip Briere
- Dr. Nick Petrella
- Juliano
- Walter J. Marshall
- Tom Freeman

Lynda Berish
Sandra Thibaudeau

UNIT 1

Pennies from Heaven

STORY 1   A GIFT FROM AN ANGEL

STORY 2   MONEY FROM THE SKY

Let's Get Ready

Read the paragraph. Write one word from the list on each line.

quarters

~~coins~~

checks

dollars

credit

Many people carry cash with them when they shop for food or clothes. They usually have some coins and some bills. The (1) ___coins___ are pennies, nickels, dimes, or (2) _____. When people carry larger amounts of money, such as ten or twenty (3) _____, they use paper money called bills. To pay for things like rent or electricity, many people write (4) _____. People also use (5) _____ cards or debit cards to pay for meals in restaurants or things they buy when they shop.

A GIFT FROM AN ANGEL

Before You Read

A. Work with a partner. Look at the picture. Talk about what you see.

B. Look at these pictures. Match each picture to a word.

A.   B.   C.   D.

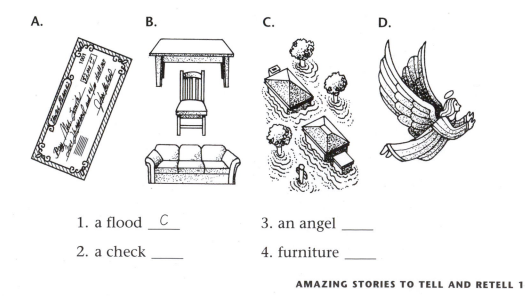

1. a flood ___C___   3. an angel _____

2. a check _____   4. furniture _____

A Gift from an Angel

In Grand Forks, North Dakota, and East Grand Forks, Minnesota, there was a big flood. There was water everywhere. Many people had water in their houses. They had to leave their homes. After the flood, they had no houses, no furniture, no clothes, and no food.

But someone decided to help. A woman decided to give money to the flood victims. She wanted to give $2,000 to each family. The woman didn't want people to know her name. People thought she was from California. They called her "Angel."

Dora was one person who got a $2,000 check. She said, "There was two feet of water in my house. I lost all my things." She and two hundred other people waited in line to get their checks. Dora said she thought an angel gave them the money.

People who worked for the city said anyone who had a flood in their house could get the money. Many people got checks for $2,000. The woman called Angel gave more than $2 million in all!

Reading Skills

READING COMPREHENSION

Reread the story. One word in each sentence below is not correct. Cross out the incorrect word. Write the correct word on each line.

1. People in Grand Forks and East Grand Forks had a ~~fire~~ in their houses. _____flood_____

2. A man wanted to give them money. _____

3. The woman didn't want people to know her address.

   _____

4. People thought Angel was from Texas. _____

5. Dora got a bill for $2,000. _____

6. Nobody who had a flood could get a check. _____

7. Angel gave people more than $2,000. _____

BUILD YOUR VOCABULARY

A. Read the sentences. Write one word from the list on each line.

money
furniture
~~water~~
family
name
check

1. A *flood* means there is too much ____water____.

2. Dora got a _____ for $2,000.

3. "Angel" didn't want people to know her _____.

4. People in the flood had no food, clothes, or _____.

5. After a flood, people need _____ to buy new things.

6. Each _____ in the flood got a check for $2,000.

B. Write your own sentences using the words listed.

1. I drink water every day. _____ .

2. _____ .

3. _____ .

4. _____ .

5. _____ .

6. _____ .

REVIEW THE INFORMATION

Which woman did these things? Put a check mark (✓) under the correct name.

	Angel	Dora
1. wanted to help	✓	
2. waited in line		
3. had water in her house		
4. got a check		
5. may live in California		
6. gave people money		
7. lost her things		
8. got $2,000		
9. lived in Grand Forks		
10. thought an angel gave the money		

Before You Read

Work with a partner. Look at the picture. Read the sentences.
Write **T** *for* **true** *or* **F** *for* **false**.

1. The truck turned over. __T__

2. There is food everywhere. ____

3. There is money everywhere. ____

4. People are putting money in their pockets. ____

5. People are sad. ____

Money from the Sky

A. One day in Overtown, Florida, $3.7 million fell from the sky. It happened when a Brinks truck turned over. There was money everywhere! One man said, "The streets were like silver." Some people took off their shirts and filled them with money.

B. Police officers went from door to door in the neighborhood. They asked people to return the money. After six hours, the total returned: zero.

C. No one in Overtown was surprised. Many people in this town are poor. They need the money to buy food for their children. They think that God sent the money to them. They say, "God sent the truck."

D. The police say this is a serious crime. "People took thousands of dollars. It's not their money, and they have to return it." The police also say it's dangerous to keep the money because everyone knows about the story from the news. People have money in their underwear drawers or their back yards, and other people will try to steal it.

E. So far, only one person has returned any money. He is a firefighter. He found $300,000 in a bag and gave it to the police. The people of Overtown still have the rest of the money.

Reading Skills

READING COMPREHENSION

Read each question. Circle the letter of the correct answer.

1. How much money fell out of the truck?
   a. $3.7 million
   b. $37 million

2. Why did the police go from door to door?
   a. to tell people about the money
   b. to ask people to return the money

3. How much money was returned?

    a. all the money

    b. $300,000

4. Where do people in Overtown say the money came from?

    a. from a bank

    b. from God

5. Why do the police say it is dangerous to keep the money?

    a. other people will come to steal the money

    b. the truck driver will get hurt

6. Who returned $300,000?

    a. a police officer

    b. a firefighter

BUILD YOUR VOCABULARY

Find the word or words in the story that mean the same as the words below. Write the story words on each line.

Paragraph A

fell on its side _turned over_ _____

Paragraph B

the area where you live _____

give back _____

Paragraph C

have very little money _____

things we eat _____

Paragraph D

places you keep your underwear _____

a place behind your house _____

to take something that is not yours _____

Paragraph E

a person who puts out fires _____

CHOOSE A TITLE

Reread this story. What is it about? Choose another title for the story. Circle the letter of the correct answer.

a. A Truck Driver's Accident

b. People Find Money and Don't Return It

c. People Keep Money in Their Back Yards

GIVE YOUR OPINION

What do you think? Read each sentence with a partner. Then write agree *or* disagree *on the line after each sentence. Talk about your answers.*

1. If people needed to buy food, it was OK to keep the money.

   _____

2. Anyone who finds money should return it. _____

3. The firefighter was stupid to return the money. _____

4. The firefighter was the only honest person. _____

5. People who keep money in their homes are in danger.

   Someone will steal it. _____

6. It is strange that only one person returned the money.

_____

7. Most people are not honest. _____

8. Anyone who returns money in a situation like this is stupid.

_____

Put It Together

LET'S REVIEW

A. Use the words below to complete the crossword puzzle. Read the stories again to help you.

poor
flood
help
Angel
crime
money
truck
check
furniture
~~returned~~
hundred

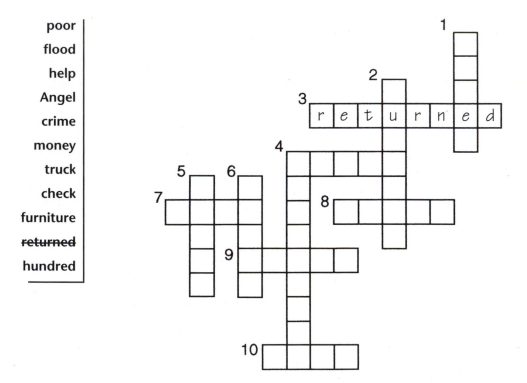

Across

3. When people found the money from the Brinks truck, only

   one person ___returned___ the money. He gave back $300,000.

4. When there is too much water, it is called a _____.

7. People who do not have very much money are _____.

8. Many people got a _____ for $2,000 from a woman
   called Angel.

9. To keep money that is not yours is a serious _____.

10. Angel gave people money because she wanted to

    _____ them.

Down

1. People called the woman from California _____
   because she wanted to help them.

2. Two _____ people waited in line to get checks.

4. People who had floods in their houses had no clothes, no

   food, and no _____.

5. Only one person returned the _____ he found.

6. One day a _____ turned over, and there was money
   everywhere.

B. Complete the chart.

	Person	Place	Action	Thing
1. in a drawer		✓		
2. money				✓
3. a police officer				
4. to work				
5. furniture				
6. to steal				
7. a woman				
8. a truck				
9. to give				
10. neighborhood				
11. child				
12. shirt				
13. a firefighter				
14. California				
15. Dora				
16. to wait				

TELL THE STORIES

A. Tell the story "A Gift from an Angel." Imagine that you are Dora and had a flood. Imagine that you call a friend who lives in another city. Use the information from the story to describe the flood, but add your own ideas as well. Tell your friend these things:

1. what happened to your house and furniture

2. how you got the money

3. what you did with the money

B. Work with a partner to tell the story "Money from the Sky." One partner takes the part of a police officer. The other partner takes the part of a person who found some money. Work on the story together. Then tell your story to a group of students in the class. Use these questions to help you.

Police officer

1. What did you see when the truck turned over?

2. What did you say when you went to people's homes to ask for the money?

3. What do you think about the people who kept the money?

Person who found the money

1. What did you see when the truck turned over?

2. Where did you put the money to take it home?

3. How much money did you take?

4. Where did you hide the money in your home?

5. Will you return the money? Why or why not?

6. If you don't return the money, how will you spend it?

TALK ABOUT IT

Discuss these questions in groups.

1. Do you know anyone who lost his or her wallet or purse? What happened?

2. Do you know anyone who found money in the street? What happened?

3. What can you use for shopping if you don't want to carry cash?

SOLVE THE PROBLEM

Discuss these situations in groups. Talk about things to do or say.

1. You are walking alone in the street and find a wallet with $500. You have a lot of bills to pay.

2. You see a man on a bike drop something out of his pocket.

3. You find a purse on the bus.

WRITING OPTION

What would you do if you had a million dollars to give away?
Write about whom you would give money to and why.

Little Heroes

STORY 1   SAVE MY MOM!

STORY 2   MY BROTHER'S IN THE DRYER!

Let's Get Ready

Read each sentence below. Circle the letter of the correct answer.

1. You call <u>911</u> for
   a. an emergency.
   b. the time.
   c. information.

2. To go to the <u>basement</u>, you go
   a. outside.
   b. upstairs.
   c. downstairs.

3. <u>Hide-and-seek</u> is a
   a. game.
   b. toy.
   c. television show.

4. A <u>dryer</u>
   a. dries dishes.
   b. dries clothes.
   c. dries food.

5. <u>Diabetes</u> is a
   a. sickness.
   b. food.
   c. part of the body.

6. <u>Paramedics</u> work
   a. in hospitals.
   b. in fire trucks.
   c. in ambulances.

Before You Read

Look at the picture. Answer the questions. Circle the letter of the correct answer.

1. How old do you think the girl is?

    a. 6 months old

    (b.) 2 years old

    c. 8 years old

2. The two people are

    a. in the bedroom.

    b. in the basement.

    c. in the kitchen.

3. The mother is

    a. unconscious.

    b. conscious.

    c. crying.

Save My Mom!

One Thursday morning, the operator at 911 emergency services was very surprised. When she answered a call, she heard a tiny voice. It was a young child. The child said, "Mommy sick, Mommy sick," over and over again.

The operator found the address of the call. She called the ambulance and the fire department. In a few minutes, the paramedics and the firefighters arrived at the house. They pushed the kitchen door open. A small voice was calling from the basement. They went down the basement stairs right away. They couldn't believe their eyes! The little girl was only two years old! She was sitting by her unconscious mother.

She was holding her mother's hand, and tears were running down the girl's cheeks.

The paramedics began giving first aid. Soon the mother opened her eyes. Then she explained what happened. "I'm Johanne Brissette," she said. "I'm diabetic. I was at the dentist. When I got back, I didn't feel well. I told Chloé, 'Mommy is sick,' and then I passed out.

"Everyone was surprised that Chloé could call 911. On Monday I tried to teach Chloé how to call 911. She couldn't do it."

The 911 operator was very surprised, too. "It's the first time I've seen a two-year-old call 911!" she said.

Reading Skills

READ FOR THE MAIN IDEA

What is this story about? Circle the letter of the correct answer.

   a. a woman is sick

   b. a little girl is in the basement

   c. a little girl saves her mother

READING COMPREHENSION

Put the story in order. Write a number on each line.

_____ The operator called the ambulance and the fire department.

_____ The paramedics gave first aid.

_1_ A little girl called 911.

_____ The paramedics saw a little girl with her unconscious mother.

_____ The paramedics heard a small voice from the basement.

_____ The mother became conscious.

GIVE THE REASONS

Match the first and second parts of each sentence.

1. The operator was surprised _C_

2. The paramedics went downstairs _____

3. The paramedics gave first aid _____

4. The mother passed out _____

5. The little girl called 911 _____

a. because her mother was sick.
b. because she was diabetic.
c. because she heard a tiny voice.
d. because the woman was unconscious.
e. because they heard a voice from the basement.

REVIEW THE VOCABULARY

A. Here are some words from the story. The letters are in the wrong order. Put the letters in the correct order. Use the information to help you.

1. hcild _____child_____   a young person

2. chkient _____   a place to cook food

3. tdentsi _____   a person who fixes teeth

4. oivec _____   something you use to speak

5. efirfghiert _____   a person who puts out fires

6. poreatro _____   a person who answers the phone at 911

7. elancambu _____   something that takes people to the hospital

8. ressadd _____   the numbers for your house

B. Write your own sentences using the words listed.

1. The child is very young. _____.

2. _____.

3. _____.

4. _____.

5. _____.

6. _____.

7. _____.

8. _____.

A.

B.

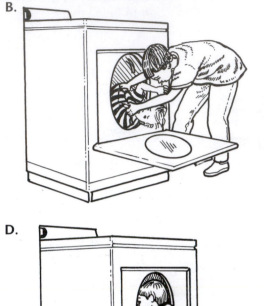

C.

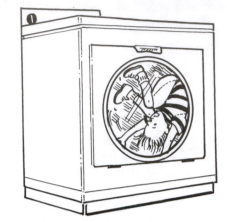

D.

Before You Read

Work with a partner. Look at the pictures. Match the pictures to the sentences. Write a letter on each line.

  __C__   A big boy hugs his little brother.

  _____   A little boy is tumbling in the dryer.

  _____   A little boy is getting into the clothes dryer.

  _____   A big boy pulls the little boy out of the dryer.

My Brother's in the Dryer!

Dustin Tarbell, 7, and his little brother David, 4 years old, were at their baby sitter's house. Suddenly, Dustin heard screams from the clothes dryer. The machine was on, and David was tumbling around inside!

Just before, Dustin and David were playing hide-and-seek with friends. There were no clothes in the dryer, and David got inside to hide. Then another child closed the door and turned the dryer on. Dustin pulled open the door of the dryer and reached inside. Usually a dryer stops when someone opens the door, but this machine was broken, and it kept turning as David screamed.

Dustin grabbed his brother's shirt. He tried to pull him out, but he couldn't. He felt his arms twist, but he hung on. Then Dustin heard his arms crack. He still didn't let go. Finally the dryer stopped, and Dustin pulled David out.

Dustin went to the hospital. He had two broken arms. But he smiled as he hugged his little brother. Kim and Robin Tarbell, the boys' parents, said they were very proud of their son Dustin. David said, "Dustin's a superhero!"

Later, the baby sitter tried to fix the dryer. He was a strong man. He tried to stop the dryer with his hands, but he couldn't stop it. Nobody could understand how a big, strong man couldn't stop the dryer, but a 7-year-old boy could. Everyone said, "It's a miracle."

Reading Skills

Reread the story. What is it about? Circle the letter of the correct answer.

a. how the dryer broke

b. how Dustin saved his brother

c. what the mother said

READING COMPREHENSION

Reread the story. Answer these questions.

1. How old was Dustin? 7 _____

2. How old was David? _____

3. Where were they? _____

4. What did Dustin hear? _____

5. What game were they playing? _____

6. Why did David get into the clothes dryer? _____

7. Who turned the dryer on? _____

8. Why did the machine keep turning? _____

9. What did Dustin do when he heard his arms crack? _____

   _____

10. What did Dustin do when the dryer stopped? _____

    _____

11. What happened to Dustin's arms? _____

12. What did David call his brother? _____

13. What happened when the baby sitter tried to stop the dryer?

    _____

USE THE INFORMATION

Who did these things? Reread the story. Write the names on each line.

1. _____David_____ called Dustin a superhero.

2. _____ stopped the dryer.

3. _____ tried to fix the dryer.

4. _____ played hide-and-seek.

5. _____ had two broken arms.

6. _____ hid in the dryer.

7. _____ screamed.

8. _____ hugged his brother.

Put It Together

LET'S REVIEW

A. Look at these pairs of words from the two stories. Do they mean the same thing? Write S if they mean the same thing. Write D if they mean different things.

1. unconscious   passed out __S__

2. small   tiny ____

3. young   old ____

4. tears   crying ____

5. twist   turn ____

6. scream   smile ____

7. proud   sad ____

8. kitchen   basement ____

9. paramedics   firefighters ____

10. first aid   help ——

11. suddenly   slowly ——

12. crack   break ——

13. right away   quickly ——

14. surprised   nervous ——

B. Match each List A item with a List B item.

List A

1. another word for *unconscious* _h_

2. a dryer ____

3. a baby sitter ____

4. a firefighter ____

5. hide-and-seek ____

6. the opposite of *start* ____

7. a room in a house ____

8. the number for emergency services ____

List B

a. a kitchen

b. 911

c. stop

d. a children's game

e. a person who puts out fires

f. a person who takes care of children

g. a machine that dries clothes

~~h.~~ passed out

TELL THE STORIES

A. Tell the story "My Brother's in the Dryer!" to a small group of students in the class. Imagine that you are the baby sitter in this story. Use these questions to help you remember the information, but use your own words to tell the story.

1. What game were the children playing?
2. Why did David get into the dryer?
3. What did Dustin hear?
4. How did Dustin pull David out of the dryer?
5. What happened to Dustin's arms?
6. What did the parents say?

B. Work in groups to act out the story "Save My Mom!" You need the following actors:

mother

little girl

operator

two paramedics or firefighters

Practice what you will say and do. Then act out the story for the class or for another group of students in the class.

TALK ABOUT IT

Discuss these questions in groups.

1. Do you have any emergency numbers near your telephone? What are they for?
2. Do you have a first aid kit or simple medical supplies at home? What is in the kit?
3. What are some emergencies that people have in the home?
4. What are some emergencies that children have?

SOLVE THE PROBLEM

Discuss these situations in groups. Talk about things to do or say. Write your ideas on a piece of paper. Then discuss your ideas with the class.

1. You see someone fall down on the street. The person is hurt and can't get up.
2. You hear a loud noise from a neighbor's apartment. Then you hear someone call, "Help!"
3. You go home at the end of the day. When you open your front door, you smell gas. There is no one in the house, but you have a cat.

IN YOUR NEIGHBORHOOD

What kinds of things are dangerous for children? Look around your neighborhood and make a list of three or four things that can be dangerous for children. Share your ideas with the class.

WRITING OPTION

Write a note to thank a neighbor who brought you lunch when you were sick for three days.

Winning the Contest

STORY 1   COURIERS IN THE COLD

STORY 2   THE BIGGEST PUMPKIN

Let's Get Ready

Work with a partner. Read these questions. Match each List A item with a List B item.

List A

1. What is a *pumpkin*? __f__

2. What do couriers do? ____

3. What is a *watermelon*? ____

4. What is a *uniform*? ____

5. What does a contest winner get? ____

6. What is another word for *giant*? ____

7. Where do we wear gloves? ____

8. What is another word for *end* or *stop*? ____

9. Which word means *very cold*? ____

10. What is a *squash*? ____

List B

a. deliver letters and packages
b. quit
c. on our hands
d. clothes we wear to work
e. a big fruit
f. a big orange vegetable
g. a green or yellow vegetable
h. a prize
i. freezing
j. big

Before You Read

A. Match the things that go together.

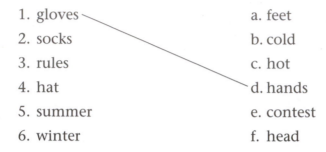

1. gloves	a. feet
2. socks	b. cold
3. rules	c. hot
4. hat	d. hands
5. summer	e. contest
6. winter	f. head

B. Work with a partner. Look at the picture on page 29. What do you know about couriers? Read the sentences. Put a check mark (✓) under True, False, or I Don't Know.

	True	False	I Don't Know
1. Couriers bring letters and packages to people.	✓		
2. Couriers wear uniforms.			
3. Couriers wear gloves in the summer.			
4. Couriers drive buses.			
5. Couriers work in summer and winter.			

C. Scan the story to check if your answers are correct.

Couriers in the Cold

Jeff Chiperzak and Shaun Finnis work as couriers. They drive trucks to deliver letters and packages to people's offices and homes.

Like all couriers, they wear uniforms to work. In summer, when the weather is hot, they wear shorts and shirts. They also wear short socks and shoes. In winter, when the weather is very cold, they wear long pants, sweaters, and jackets. They wear gloves on their hands and warm hats on their heads, too.

One day last May, Jeff and Shaun decided to start a contest.

They wanted to see who could wear his summer uniform the longest. They asked other couriers to be in the contest. The rules were simple: the couriers had to wear shorts and short socks. They could not wear pants, long socks, or sweaters.

There were six couriers in the contest. In October, the weather started to get cold. Two couriers quit the contest, but Jeff and Shaun didn't quit. Jeff said, "My hands were very cold, so I started to wear gloves." Shaun said, "My knees were freezing," but he didn't wear long pants. By November, the temperature was very cold. One day, it was minus 30 degrees, but Jeff and Shaun didn't quit. In December, Jeff and Shaun were still wearing short pants. When people received their Christmas packages, they were really surprised to see their couriers in short pants!

Jeff and Shaun didn't want to end the contest, and one year later they are still in short pants. Now some new couriers want to join the contest.

Reading Skills

Reread the story. Answer these questions.

1. What work do Jeff and Shaun do? <u>They are couriers.</u>

2. How do they deliver letters and packages? _____

3. What do couriers wear to work? _____

4. What were the rules of the contest? _____

   _____

5. How many couriers were in the contest at first? _____

6. What was the temperature in November? _____

7. Why were people surprised when they got their Christmas

   packages? _____

8. What are Jeff and Shaun wearing one year later? _____

   _____

BUILD YOUR VOCABULARY

A. Match the words and pictures.

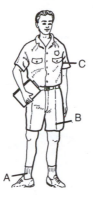 

Summer uniform	Winter uniform
1. shorts ___B___	5. gloves ____
2. jacket ____	6. sweater ____
3. shirt ____	7. short socks ____
4. long pants ____	8. long socks ____

B. Complete the lists of the couriers' summer clothes and winter clothes.

Summer	Winter
shorts	long pants
_____	_____
_____	_____
_____	_____
_____	_____
_____	_____
_____	_____

Before You Read

Work with a partner. Read each question below. Circle the letter of the correct answer.

1. Which of these is the biggest?

   a. a pumpkin

   b. an apple

   c. a cantaloupe

2. Which of these is the smallest?

   a. an apple

   b. a grape

   c. an orange

3. Which of these is the sweetest?

   a. an apple

   b. a lemon

   c. candy

4. Which of these is the sourest?

   a. a grapefruit

   b. a lemon

   c. an orange

5. Which of these has the most seeds?

   a. an apple

   b. a grapefruit

   c. a watermelon

6. Which of these is the most expensive?

   a. an apple

   b. a lemon

   c. a pineapple

The Biggest Pumpkin

People started to grow big pumpkins more than 100 years ago. About 20 years ago, Howard Dill decided to have a contest. He brought his biggest pumpkin to the contest. It weighed 438 pounds. Every year, people brought bigger pumpkins. Two years ago, another pumpkin grower set a world record. His pumpkin weighed 1,061 pounds!

One of the pumpkin contests is at a festival called Pumpkinfest. At Pumpkinfest, people bring giant pumpkins and other giant vegetables. There is a contest for the biggest watermelon and the biggest squash. There is even a contest for the world's biggest flowers. Many of the giant fruits and vegetables weigh more than 500 pounds. Some of the flowers are more than 14 feet high!

At Pumpkinfest, people walk around and look at the giant fruits and vegetables. They can even buy them after the contest and take them home. "There is only one problem," said a man who bought a giant pumpkin. "I can't get the pumpkin into my truck!"

Have you ever seen a 1,000-pound pumpkin? Howard Dill has. He is a world champion pumpkin grower. Most pumpkins weigh from 15 to 30 pounds, but Howard Dill has giant pumpkins that weigh much more. Every year, he meets other pumpkin growers from across North America. They have contests to see who can grow the biggest pumpkin. The winners get prizes, such as money or trips to exciting places.

Reading Skills

Read these sentences. Write T *for* **true** *or* F *for* **false.**

1. Howard Dill grows very big pumpkins. _T_

2. Every year, there are contests to see who has the biggest pumpkin. _____

3. People have been growing giant pumpkins for 10 years. _____

4. Every year, the pumpkins are the same size. _____

5. One pumpkin was more than 1,000 pounds. _____

6. At Pumpkinfest, there are contests for giant fruits, vegetables, and animals. _____

7. People can only look at the giant fruits and vegetables. _____

8. One man couldn't get a giant pumpkin into his truck. _____

BUILD YOUR VOCABULARY

Here are some prizewinning fruits and vegetables. Make separate lists of the fruits and vegetables. Put them in order from biggest to smallest.

The Biggest Fruits and Vegetables

apple	3 pounds	potato	7½ pounds
cabbage	124 pounds	pumpkin	994 pounds
cantaloupe	55 pounds	pineapple	28¾ pounds
carrot	15 pounds	radish	28 pounds
cucumber	17 pounds	squash	672 pounds
grapefruit	6½ pounds	strawberry	8½ pounds
lemon	8 pounds	tomato	7¾ pounds
melon	59½ pounds	watermelon	279 pounds
onion	10¼ pounds	zucchini	64 pounds

	Fruits	Vegetables
1.	watermelon	
2.		
3.		
4.		
5.		
6.		
7.		
8.		
9.	apple	

MAKE COMPARISONS

To compare two things, you add *er* to short adjectives such as *big* and *small (bigger, smaller).*

Read these sentences. Look at the chart in the previous exercise. Write bigger *or* smaller *on each line below.*

1. The watermelon is _____smaller_____ than the pumpkin.

2. The zucchini is _____ than the onion.

3. The apple is _____ than the carrot.

4. The cantaloupe is _____ than the cabbage.

5. The tomato is _____ than the pineapple.

6. The potato is _____ than the radish.

7. The melon is _____ than the lemon.

8. The grapefruit is _____ than the cucumber.

9. The lemon is _____ than the radish.

10. The watermelon is _____ than the onion.

Put It Together

LET'S REVIEW

Match the first and second parts of each sentence.

1. Jeff and Shaun decided to start a contest _*b*_

2. There were six couriers _____

3. The average pumpkin weighs _____

4. Some giant flowers _____

5. Jeff started to wear gloves _____

6. One day in November, _____

7. The biggest pumpkin weighed _____

8. Pumpkinfest has contests _____

a. 1,061 pounds.

b. last May.

c. are more than 14 feet high.

d. in the contest.

e. between 15 and 30 pounds.

f. it was minus 30 degrees.

g. because his hands were freezing.

h. for giant fruits and vegetables.

TELL THE STORIES

A. Tell the story "Couriers in the Cold" to another student in the class. First draw pictures of the couriers in their winter uniforms and in their summer uniforms. Then use the pictures to help you explain the story. Use these questions to help you remember the information, but use your own words to tell the story.

1. What kind of work do couriers do?
2. Who decided to have a contest?
3. What were the rules of the contest?
4. Who won the contest?

B. Tell the story "The Biggest Pumpkin." To practice, tell the story to another student in the class. Then tell the story to a friend or some-one in your family after class. Use these questions to help you re-member the information, but use your own words to tell the story.

1. How much does an average pumpkin weigh?
2. How much did the biggest pumpkin weigh?
3. What is Pumpkinfest?
4. What other vegetables do people bring to Pumpkinfest?
5. What are some things you can do and see at Pumpkinfest?

First, tell the story to someone outside of class. Then ask them these questions:

1. Did you ever enter a contest? _____
2. What did you do in the contest? _____
3. Do you know who won the contest? _____
4. What was the prize? _____

TALK ABOUT IT

Discuss these questions in groups.

1. Why do people start contests?
2. What are good prizes for contests?
3. Are there any contests that can be dangerous?
4. Are there any contests where you can lose money?
5. What kinds of contests are the most fun?
6. How often do you or your friends enter contests?
7. Do you know anyone who has won a prize in a contest? What was the prize?
8. How do people feel if they lose in a contest?

SOLVE THE PROBLEM

Work in groups. Think of a contest that you can have in your class or in your school. The contest must follow these rules.

1. The contest must be educational. For example, it can be a contest to see who can read the fastest or who can spell the most words in English.
2. The contest should be fun.
3. Everyone in the class must be able to be in the contest.
4. The contest should not be dangerous.
5. There should be no money involved in the contest.
6. There can be a small prize.
7. No one's feelings should get hurt because of the contest.

Talk about the contest ideas from each group. Choose the most interesting contest to have in your class or in your school. You can have the contest at the beginning or end of class or after class.

IN YOUR NEIGHBORHOOD

What kinds of contests are there in your neighborhood? Make a list of several contests. Say what store or club started the contest, what the prize was, and who won it.

WRITING OPTION

Look at the questions in Talk About It *on page 38. Write the answers to some or all of these questions.*

UNIT 4

Animal Encounters

STORY 1   THE ENGINE THAT PURRED

STORY 2   ALLIGATOR ATTACK!

Let's Get Ready

A. Match the words and pictures.

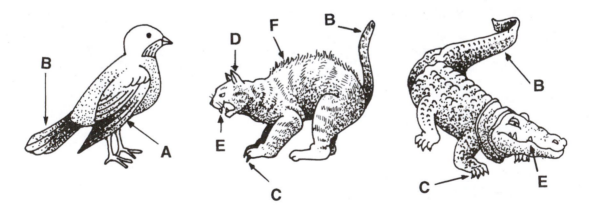

1. claw __C__   4. ear _____

2. teeth _____   5. fur _____

3. tail _____   6. wing _____

B. Work with a partner. Complete the chart.

	Cats	Birds	Alligators	Dogs	Fish
1. have tails and fur	✓			✓	
2. are popular pets					
3. live in the water					
4. live in hot places					
5. have claws					
6. have wings					
7. have big teeth					
8. are green or brown					
9. are many different colors					
10. people eat them					

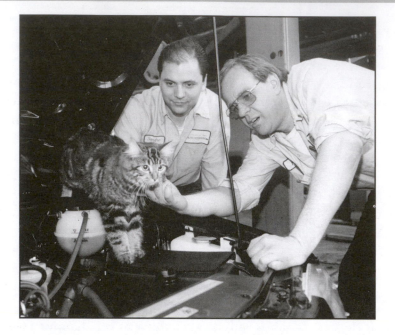

Before You Read

Look at the picture. Work with a partner. Discuss these questions.

1. What kind of animal do you see?

2. Where is it?

3. Why do you think it is there?

The Engine That Purred

Sandro Ravazzano works in a garage as a car mechanic. One morning, he opened the hood of a car and got a big surprise. A cat was sitting on the engine! "I jumped when I opened the hood," he said. "Sometimes you see rats or birds in a car. When they get into the engine, they die. This cat was lucky. I think it was too scared to move. That's why it's still alive."

The cat was in a 1995 Volkswagen Jetta. The owner of the Jetta had a long drive to get to the garage, so everyone was very surprised that the cat was alive. Sandro called the owner of the car. The car owner was very surprised to hear about the cat. "I don't even have a cat," he said.

No one knew where the cat came from, but the car owner had an idea. "Maybe it's my neighbor's cat. But it's funny that I didn't hear anything. The cat didn't even meow!"

Everyone in the garage liked the cat. They named her Jetta. "She's cute and friendly," they said. They gave her some milk, and someone went out to buy cat food. Then the car owner came and took the cat home. He knocked on all the doors in the neighborhood. Finally he found the woman who had lost the cat. She was very happy to see her cat. "I was so worried because my cat was missing," she said. "Thank you for finding her!" The cat just purred.

Reading Skills

READING COMPREHENSION

A. Check (✓) the things that are true.

1. Sandro works as a mechanic. __✓__

2. A cat was under the car. _____

3. The cat was alive. _____

4. The car was a 1998 Jetta. _____

5. The car owner lived near the garage. ____

6. The car owner was looking for his cat. ____

7. The people in the garage liked the cat. ____

8. The woman was happy to see her cat. ____

B. Put the story in order. Write a number on each line.

____ The car owner said, "I don't even have a cat."

_1_ Sandro opened the hood of a car.

____ The people in the garage gave the cat some milk.

____ A cat was sitting on the engine.

____ Sandro called the owner of the car.

____ The cat owner was happy to see her cat.

REVIEW THE VOCABULARY

One word in each group doesn't belong. Cross out that word.

Car	Cat	People	Feelings
garage	milk	scared	happy
engine	meow	mechanic	scared
hood	garage	neighbor	engine
~~surprise~~	food	owner	surprised

UNDERSTAND THE PRONOUNS

Read each sentence. Write the word or words that mean the same as the underlined word.

the cat's
owner

the people
in the
garage

~~Sandro~~

the cat

the car
owner

rats or
birds

1. "I jumped when I opened the hood," <u>he</u> said. _____Sandro_____

2. <u>They</u> get into the engine. _____

3. <u>It</u> was too scared to move. _____

4. "I don't even have a cat," <u>he</u> said. _____

5. <u>They</u> named her Jetta. _____

6. "Thank you for finding my cat," <u>she</u> said. _____

Before You Read

Work with a partner. Look at the picture. Answer these questions.

1. Where are the people?

2. What animal do you see?

3. What do you think will happen?

Alligator Attack!

Loretta Keith was camping in Florida with her five-year-old son, Michael, her friend Susie, and Susie's two young daughters. They decided to take a canoe trip. On this kind of trip, people relax as they paddle their canoes slowly down the river. At the end of the trip, the park people pick them up. Everyone told them it was very safe.

It was a beautiful, hot day. Everyone was having fun. They were looking at the plants and fish in the water. Suddenly, they heard a noise. Susie said, "Don't worry, it's only a big fish. Then they heard a louder sound: Splash! Loretta knew what it was. It was an alligator!

All of a sudden, the canoe began to rise out of the water. Then they saw the alligator. It was huge! It was swimming under the canoe. Loretta screamed, "Don't anybody move!" The alligator was as big as the canoe. It scratched Loretta's hand with its claws when it turned over in the water. Then another alligator came out. Everyone was afraid to move or speak.

Loretta grabbed the paddle and rowed back to shore as fast as she could. When they got to shore, everyone was shaking, but the park people smiled. They said, "It wasn't dangerous. Alligators don't hurt you if you don't hurt them." Loretta answered, "I hit it on the head with the paddle. I think I hurt it." Everyone laughed, and Loretta said, "We'll never forget how scared we were when we saw the alligators under our canoe!"

Reading Skills

READING COMPREHENSION

Read the questions. Write the answers on the lines.

1. Where was Loretta Keith camping? _____ in Florida _____

2. Who was with her? _____

_____

3. What did everyone tell them about the trip?

_____

4. What did they hear? _____

5. What did they see when the canoe began to rise? _____

_____

6. How big was the alligator? _____

7. How did it scratch Loretta's hand? _____

8. How did everyone feel? _____

9. What did Loretta do? _____

_____

10. What did the park people say about alligators? _____

_____

11. How did Loretta hurt the alligator? _____

_____

READING COMPREHENSION

*Which thing happened first? Read each pair of sentences, then number them **1** or **2**.*

1. __2__ They decided to take a canoe trip.

   __1__ Loretta Keith was camping in Florida with her friends.

2. ____ They were looking at plants and fish in the water.

   ____ They heard some noise.

3. ____ They saw an alligator.

   ____ The canoe began to rise.

4. _____ The alligator scratched Loretta's hand.

   _____ Another alligator came out.

5. _____ Loretta turned the canoe around.

   _____ Loretta took the paddle.

6. _____ The park people smiled at them.

   _____ They got to the shore.

REVIEW THE VOCABULARY

Who or what did these things? Put a check mark (✓) in the correct place.

	Park People	Loretta	Alligator
1. turned the canoe around		✓	
2. scratched Loretta's hand			
3. made a big sound			
4. screamed			
5. said it wasn't dangerous			
6. smiled at Loretta			
7. turned over in the water			
8. took the paddle			
9. hurt the alligator			
10. decided to take a canoe trip			

Put It Together

A. Read the paragraph. Write one word from the list on each line.

milk
~~hood~~
engine
alive
garage
surprised
neighbor's
owner

One day Sandro Ravazzano opened the (1) _____hood_____ of a car and saw a cat sitting on the (2) _____. He was very (3) _____ that the cat was (4) _____. He called the (5) _____ of the car. The owner said, "Maybe it's my (6) _____ cat." The people in the (7) _____ gave the cat some (8) _____. Then the car owner took the cat home to her owner.

B. Read the paragraph. Write one word from the list on each line.

afraid
~~canoe~~
Splash
hurt
hand
camping
safe
alligator

Loretta and her friends were in a (1) _____canoe_____. They were (2) _____ in Florida. Everyone told them it was very (3) _____. Suddenly, they heard a big sound: (4) _____! They saw a huge (5) _____. The alligator scratched Loretta's (6) _____. Everyone was (7) _____ to move or speak. Then Loretta turned the canoe around and went back to shore. The park people said, "Alligators don't hurt you if you don't hurt them." Loretta said, "I think I (8) _____ it!"

C. Choose eight words from the lists on page 50. Write a sentence for each word.

1. _____

2. _____

3. _____

4. _____

5. _____

6. _____

7. _____

8. _____

TELL THE STORIES

A. Work in groups of three to tell the story "The Engine That Purred" or "Alligator Attack!"

Step 1: Together, choose one story and write the story in your own words.

Step 2: Cut the story into strips. Put one or two sentences on each strip.

Step 3: Give the strips to another group of students. Ask them to put the story in order.

B. Work in groups to act out the story "Alligator Attack!" Imagine that you are in another canoe and the alligators attack you, too. Two or three students can be passengers in the canoe. Act out what you say and do when you see the alligator under your canoe.

TALK ABOUT IT

Discuss these questions in groups.

1. Do you have a pet? What is it?
2. When did you get the pet?
3. Which animals make good pets?
4. Were you ever near an animal in the wild?
5. What happened? Were you surprised or afraid? What did you do?

SOLVE THE PROBLEM

Discuss these situations in groups. Talk about things to do or say.

1. Your neighbor in the next apartment shows you his new pet. It is a small boa constrictor.
2. You find a baby bird in the woods. You don't see its mother. You think the bird is hungry.
3. There is a skunk under your porch.
4. At the zoo, you see a child put her hand in a bear's cage.

IN YOUR NEIGHBORHOOD

What kind of animals live in your neighborhood? Work in groups. Describe three animals in your neighborhood. What do the animals look like? How often do you see these animals?

WRITING OPTION

Describe a pet that you or someone you know has. What kind of animal is it? What does it look like? What does it eat? What are its good and bad points?

A Helping Hand

STORY 1   THE TEDDY BEAR LADY

STORY 2   DRESSING FOR SUCCESS

Let's Get Ready

A. Work with a partner. Read these questions. Write the letter of the correct answer on each line.

Who or what . . .

1. has a million dollars? __h__

2. works without getting paid? ____

3. has a lot of money? ____

4. works in an office? ____

5. is a toy? ____

6. is a place for sick people? ____

7. does someone wear to work? ____

8. do you have before you get a job? ____

a. a secretary
b. a job interview
c. a hospital
d. a rich person
e. a teddy bear
f. a suit
g. a volunteer
h. a millionaire

Before You Read

Look at the picture. Read each sentence. Circle the letter of the correct answer.

1. The woman who is sitting is a
   a. teacher.
   b. secretary.
2. The man who is standing is the
   a. boss.
   b. student.
3. They are in
   a. an office.
   b. a hospital.

The Teddy Bear Lady

Gladys Holm was a secretary. She worked in an office all her life. Gladys earned about $15,000 a year. She died when she was 86 years old. And she left a big surprise—$18 million! She gave the money to a children's hospital.

Gladys Holm never got married or had any children. But she always liked children, and she wanted to help them. When her friend's daughter was sick in the hospital, Gladys brought her a teddy bear. After that, she visited the hospital many times. Every time she visited, she brought teddy bears for the sick children. After a while, people started to call Gladys the "Teddy Bear Lady."

Gladys always gave toys and gifts to her friends and family, but no one knew she had a lot of money. She lived in a small house outside of Chicago. Everyone was very surprised when they learned she was a millionaire. A family friend said, "She always gave us nice gifts and things, but we didn't know she was rich."

How did Gladys get so much money? She asked her boss how to invest her money, and she listened to his advice. She bought the stocks that he told her to buy, and she got very rich. Before she died, she talked to her friends about "giving something to the children's hospital." No one knew that the "something" was $18 million!

Reading Skills

READ FOR THE MAIN IDEA

Reread the story. What is it about? Circle the letter of the correct answer.

    a. how Gladys Holm helped sick children

    b. where Gladys Holm lived

    c. where Gladys Holm worked

READING COMPREHENSION

Match the first and second parts of each sentence.

1. Gladys Holm worked __b__	a. that Gladys had so much money.
2. When she died, she left ____	b. as a secretary.
3. She brought teddy bears ____	c. because she listened to her boss's advice.
4. People started to call Gladys ____	d. to sick children in the hospital.
5. Everyone was surprised ____	e. the "Teddy Bear Lady."
6. Gladys got rich ____	f. $18 million.

BUILD YOUR VOCABULARY

A. Read the sentences. Write one word from the list on each line.

rich

hospital

teddy bear

~~secretary~~

earn

boss

millionaire

stocks

1. A __secretary__ works in an office.

2. Sick people are in a _____ .

3. A person who has a million dollars is a _____ .

4. People invest money in _____ .

5. People who work _____ money.

6. A _____ is a kind of toy.

56

7. A person in an office who tells you what to do is a

   _____ .

8. People with a lot of money are _____ .

B. *Write your own sentences using the words listed above.*

1. _____

   _____ .

2. _____

   _____ .

3. _____

   _____ .

4. _____

   _____ .

5. _____

   _____ .

6. _____

   _____ .

7. _____

   _____ .

8. _____

   _____ .

Before You Read

Look at the list of clothes. Where do people wear each thing?
Complete the chart. Some things can go in more than one place.

	Job Interview	Party	Home
1. a business suit	✓		
2. a skirt			
3. a T-shirt			
4. a blouse			
5. a sweater			
6. jeans			
7. a bathrobe			
8. sneakers			
9. high-heeled shoes			

Dressing for Success

Patricia was worried. She had a job interview, and she wanted to look good. She decided to get some new clothes. The store owner, Pallas Hansen, helped Patricia find a suit. But when she left the store, she didn't pay for the suit!

How could Patricia do this? She was in a special store called Career Closet in San Jose, California. Pallas Hansen and Charlotte Krumwiede started this nonprofit store to help women. They knew that many women don't find jobs because they don't have the right clothes for a job interview. Women who don't have a lot of money have to use their money to buy food and clothes for their children. They can't buy clothes for themselves.

Pallas and Charlotte started the store in 1992 after they heard about a store like this in Chicago. Volunteers work in the store. Working women donate most of the clothes to the store. This makes it possible for the customers at Career Closet to get clothes for free.

Career Closet has helped 2,500 San Jose women. But clothes aren't the only things women get at the store. They also get confidence. Patricia is 36 years old. Her husband was hurt in an accident, and Patricia needed a job to support her seven children. She went to Career Closet and got a jacket, a skirt, and a blouse. "The whole day made me feel special," she said. Patricia was a success at her interview, and she got the job. One reason she got it was because she was wearing the right clothes for the workplace.

Pallas says, "I love this job. Sixty percent of the women get jobs. It's like being a fairy godmother."

Reading Skills

Find the words that mean the same as the underlined words.
Circle the letter of the correct answer.

1. Pallas Hansen started this <u>nonprofit store</u> to help women.

   a. a store where people make money

   b. a store where people don't make money

2. <u>Volunteers</u> work in the store.

   a. people who are paid

   b. people who are not paid

3. Working women <u>donate</u> most of the clothes to the store.

   a. give

   b. sell

4. The women who visit the store <u>get confidence.</u>

   a. feel good about themselves

   b. feel afraid

5. Patricia needed a job to <u>support</u> her seven children.

   a. help her children stand up

   b. buy food and clothes for her children

6. It's like being a <u>fairy godmother.</u>

   a. a grandmother

   b. a person who helps other people

READING COMPREHENSION

Read the sentences. Write **T** *for* **true** *or* **F** *for* **false.** *Correct wrong information.*

1. Patricia got a suit. _____T_____

2. Patricia wanted to look good for a job interview.

   _____

3. Patricia paid for her clothes. _____

4. Career Closet doesn't make money from the clothes it has.

   _____

5. Some women can't find jobs because they don't dress well for

   job interviews. _____

6. There is another Career Closet in Chicago. _____

7. Pallas and Charlotte get clothes for Career Closet from a

   factory. _____

8. People who work in the store don't get paid. _____

9. Patricia felt good when she got the clothes at Career Closet.

   _____

10. Pallas likes to help other women. _____

REVIEW THE VOCABULARY

Read the definitions. Write one word from the list on each line.

owner
donate
interview
~~volunteer~~
support
confident

1. a person who helps other people and doesn't get paid

   volunteer

2. to give clothes or other things _____

3. to earn money for your family _____

4. feeling happy and hopeful _____

5. a meeting to get a job _____

6. a person who has a store or business _____

Put It Together

LET'S REVIEW

A. Review these words from the unit. Cross out the word in each group that doesn't belong.

1. secretary   boss   ~~car~~   office

2. donate   volunteer   stocks   nonprofit

3. suit   blouse   store   jacket

4. money   family   rich   millionaire

5. work   friend   job   interview

6. teddy bear   married   gift   toy

7. woman   husband   children   suit

B. Read this paragraph. Then close your book and write each sentence as your teacher dictates it.

Some people are special because they help other people. Some people give money to hospitals or other places. Other people give things such as clothes or toys. People also help others when they make someone smile.

TELL THE STORIES

A. Tell the story "The Teddy Bear Lady" to a group of students in the class. Imagine that you work at the children's hospital and you just received $18 million for the hospital. Use your own words to tell the story. Use these questions to help you.

1. Where did Gladys Holm work?
2. How did she help sick children?
3. How did she get her money?
4. Why were the people at the hospital surprised to receive so much money?

Add your own ending to the story. Explain how the hospital will use the money.

B. Write the story "Dressing for Success" in your own words to help you remember the information. Then tell the story to your teacher or to another student in the class. Don't look at the story when you speak. Use your own words.
When you tell the story, change one thing—information about Pallas Hansen or information about Patricia. See if he or she can find the thing you changed.

TALK ABOUT IT

Discuss these questions in groups.

1. Why do people choose to do volunteer work?
2. What are some volunteer organizations you know about?
3. What kinds of work do they do?

4. Would you like to be a volunteer? Why or why not?

5. Do you know anyone who works as a volunteer? What does he or she do?

SOLVE THE PROBLEM

Discuss these situations in groups. Talk about things to do.

1. There is a big fire in your neighborhood and some families have no homes.

2. You have a lot of money to give to charities. You have to choose which charities you will give it to.

IN YOUR NEIGHBORHOOD

Talk to friends and neighbors about organizations in your community that ask for donations of clothing, furniture, or other things. Share this information with the class.

WRITING OPTION

Write an advertisement to ask for volunteers at a hospital. Use this information in your ad.

3–6 hours a week   work in the gift shop

help patients with meals   visit lonely people

Lifestyles

STORY 1   A YEAR WITHOUT TV

STORY 2   BUY NOTHING DAY

Let's Get Ready

A. Read these questions. Then walk around the room and ask students the questions. When someone answers "yes" to a question, write his or her name on the line.

Do you like to . . .

1. watch more than two hours of TV every day? _____

2. go shopping? _____

3. cook? _____

4. play the piano? _____

5. watch music videos? _____

6. watch TV only on the weekends? _____

7. buy a lot of Christmas gifts? _____

8. listen to tapes or compact disks? _____

9. play computer games? _____

10. play cards? _____

11. read the newspaper every day? _____

12. buy a lot of birthday gifts? _____

Before You Read

TV
love
cards
reading
mother
boy
evening
father
parents
year
day
night
happy
computer
games
like
bored

A. Complete the chart. Write each word in the correct place.

People	Entertainment	Time	Feelings
	TV		

B. Discuss this question in a group: What are your favorite pastimes? Choose activities from the list below or add your own ideas. Give information about the things you like to do. For example, if you play a sport, explain what sport you play and why you like it.

watching TV

watching movies

going shopping

playing sports

talking on the telephone

listening to music

playing games

reading

eating out

doing a hobby

using a computer

playing music

A Year without TV

Ryan Ruby is ten years old. He loves to watch TV. But for one full year, he did not watch TV at all. What was the reason? Ryan's parents said they would give him $600 if he didn't watch TV for a year.

Ryan's parents thought he watched too much TV. One day his mother saw a newspaper story about a boy who didn't watch TV for a year. She showed the story to Ryan. "It was a joke," his mother said. "I didn't think he would do it." But Ryan liked the idea. He turned off the TV right away. He said, "It doesn't bother me not to watch TV. I just want the money."

At first, Ryan's parents were very happy. Ryan read the newspaper, played outside, played computer games, and played cards with his mother. But after a while, he got bored. Every evening, he asked his parents, "What are we doing tonight?" Sometimes his mother and father wished he would watch TV, just for one evening. Ryan always said, "No, it would cost me money!"

Finally the year was over. Then Ryan started watching his favorite TV shows all day long again. Ryan got the money from his parents. What does he plan to do with the $600? "I want to buy myself a TV set!" he said.

Reading Skills

Match the first and second parts of each sentence.

1. Ryan didn't watch TV for one year _g_

2. Ryan's parents said they would give him $600 ____

3. Ryan's parents were happy at first ____

4. When Ryan got bored, ____

5. Ryan's parents sometimes wished ____

6. When the year was over, ____

7. Ryan wants to use the money ____

a. that Ryan would watch TV for one evening.
b. to buy himself a TV.
c. if he didn't watch TV for a year.
d. he asked his parents, "What are we doing tonight?"
e. because Ryan read the newspaper and played games.
f. Ryan watched TV shows all day.
g. because he wanted the $600.

SENTENCE STUDY

Match the sentences that mean the same thing.

1. "It doesn't bother me not to watch TV." _b_

2. After a while, he got bored. ____

3. His mother and father wished he would watch TV. ____

4. "It would cost me money." ____

a. He watched the shows he liked the most.
b. "It's not important to me to watch TV."
c. After a while, he wasn't having fun.
d. His parents wanted him to watch TV.
e. "I would not get all of the $600."
f. What will he buy with the money?

5. Ryan watched his favorite

   shows. ____

6. What does he plan to do with the

   money? ____

GIVE YOUR OPINION

What do you think? Read each sentence with a partner. Then write agree *or* disagree *on the line after each sentence. Talk about your answers.*

1. Most children watch too much TV. _____

2. It's a good idea to give children money so they won't watch

   TV. _____

3. Children should play outside every day. _____

4. Many children get bored if they can't watch TV. _____

5. It is OK for children to watch a lot of TV. _____

6. Children should have their own TV if they want to.

   _____

Before You Read

A. Work with a partner. Look at the picture. Talk about what you see.

B. Write this year's dates for these holidays. You can check a calendar if you don't remember the dates.

1. Christmas _____ Dec. 25 _____

2. Thanksgiving _____

3. Easter _____

4. Mother's Day _____

5. Memorial Day _____

6. Good Friday _____

7. Presidents' Day _____

8. Labor Day _____

9. Independence Day _____

10. Valentine's Day _____

11. Columbus Day _____

12. Father's Day _____

13. Veterans Day _____

14. Martin Luther King Day _____

15. St. Patrick's Day _____

16. New Year's Day _____

C. Work in groups. Choose one holiday that is important to you. Talk about what you do on that day.

Buy Nothing Day

Most people buy a lot of gifts just before Christmas. But some people think we buy too much. They have started a special day called Buy Nothing Day. They don't want anyone to go shopping on that day.

Buy Nothing Day is November 29. It's 25 days before Christmas. It's after Thanksgiving and often the first day of Christmas shopping. At this time, we see ads in newspapers and on TV telling us to "buy, buy, buy!"

The idea for Buy Nothing Day started in Vancouver, British Columbia. Now people all over the world celebrate Buy Nothing Day. In California, parents and children get together to read stories, sing songs, and paint pictures. The children talk about why they don't need a lot of toys. This year, in Manchester, England, people dressed up in costumes to tell people that we buy too much.

In Albuquerque, New Mexico, high school students wanted to tell other students about Buy Nothing Day. They organized a spaghetti dinner to give people information about Buy Nothing Day. They asked restaurants in the neighborhood to donate the food. They made posters and talked to other students about it. The dinner was a big success, and many students agreed not to buy anything on November 29. The students at the high school liked the idea of this new tradition. Next year, they want to have another dinner to tell more people about Buy Nothing Day!

Reading Skills

READING COMPREHENSION

Reread the story and answer the questions. Write the answers on the lines.

1. When is Buy Nothing Day? _____November 29_____

2. What do we see in ads after Thanksgiving? _____

_____

3. Where did the idea start? _____

4. What did parents and children in California do for Buy Nothing Day? _____

   _____

5. What did people in Manchester, England, want to tell people?

   _____

6. Why did students in New Mexico organize a spaghetti dinner?

   _____

7. Where did they get the food for their dinner? _____

   _____

8. What did many students agree to do after the dinner?

   _____

BUILD YOUR VOCABULARY

Match each list A item with a list B item.

List A

1. sing _e_
2. read ____
3. paint ____
4. donate ____
5. make ____
6. talk ____
7. celebrate ____
8. agree ____

List B

a. posters
b. food
c. to buy nothing
d. stories
e. songs
f. pictures
g. to people
h. Buy Nothing Day

REVIEW THE VOCABULARY

Complete the chart.

	Holiday	Place	Person	Thing
1. Christmas	✓			
2. toy				✓
3. Vancouver				
4. poster				
5. parent				
6. Manchester				
7. Thanksgiving				
8. child				
9. spaghetti dinner				
10. New Mexico				
11. high school student				
12. Buy Nothing Day				
13. newspaper				
14. California				
15. picture				
16. British Columbia				

Put It Together

Make six sentences using the words from Lists A, B, and C.

List A	List B	List C
~~Ryan Ruby~~	tell people to buy things	on November 29.
Newspaper ads	celebrate Buy Nothing Day	his favorite TV shows.
Every evening, Ryan Ruby	~~didn't watch TV~~	or read the newspaper.
Students in New Mexico	Ryan watched	to tell people about Buy Nothing Day.
People in many countries	had a spaghetti dinner	before Christmas.
When the year was over,	played games	~~for one year.~~

1. Ryan Ruby didn't watch TV for one year.

2. _____

_____

3. _____

_____

4. _____

_____

5. _____

_____

6. _____

_____

TELL THE STORIES

A. Tell the story "A Year without TV." Imagine that you are Ryan Ruby's mother or father. To practice, tell the story to another student in the class. Then tell the story to a friend or someone in your family after class. Use these questions to help you remember the information, but use your own words to tell the story.

1. Why did you want Ryan to stop watching TV?

2. Why did Ryan decide not to watch TV?

3. What did Ryan do every evening when he didn't watch TV?

4. How did you feel when Ryan didn't watch TV?

5. At the end of the year, do you think it was a good idea to pay Ryan not to watch TV?

6. Would you suggest this idea to other parents?

After you tell the story to another person, ask him or her this question: **Do you think it was a good idea for Ryan's parents to give him money to stop watching TV? Why or why not?** *Share this information with the class.*

B. Work with a partner to tell the story "Buy Nothing Day." One partner takes the part of a small store owner. The other partner takes the part of a high school student in Albuquerque, New Mexico. Work on the story together. Then tell your story to a group of students in the class.

Store owner

You own a small store. On November 29, no one comes into your store to buy anything. Explain how you feel about Buy Nothing Day.

Student

You are a high school student who helped organize the spaghetti dinner for Buy Nothing Day. You think that people buy too many things. Explain about Buy Nothing Day and how you feel about it.

TALK ABOUT IT

Discuss these questions in groups.

1. How many hours of TV do you watch each week?
2. What are your favorite TV shows?
3. How much TV do you think children should watch each week?
4. How often do you go shopping?
5. What kinds of things do you shop for?
6. Do you think people shop too much? Why or why not?

SOLVE THE PROBLEM

Discuss these situations in groups. Talk about things to do or say.

1. You think that your friend's child watches too much TV every day. You think the child should play outside more.
2. Your friend goes shopping a lot. She buys a lot of things that you think are not very important. She often asks you for money to buy coffee or a sandwich because she has no money left.
3. There are some shows on TV that you like to watch. The people in your family don't like these shows. They like to watch other shows. Every day, people in your family fight about which shows to watch.

IN YOUR NEIGHBORHOOD

Look at a calendar to see which big holiday is next. In your neighborhood, look in stores or in newspapers. What kinds of advertisements do you see for this holiday? Share this information with the class.

WRITING OPTION

Work in groups of three to design posters for Buy Nothing Day.

UNIT 7

At Home

STORY 1   HOME, SWEET HOME

STORY 2   STUCK ON DUCT TAPE

Let's Get Ready

Match the words and pictures

A.

B.

C.

D.

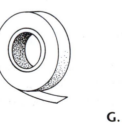

E.

F.

G.

1. a pail and shovel ___D___   5. tape ____

2. a beehive ____   6. honey ____

3. to dig ____   7. a roof ____

4. a wallet ____

77

HOME, SWEET HOME

Before You Read

A. Look at the picture. Work with a partner. Check (✓) the things you see.

1. bees ___✓___

2. a wall _____

3. a pail _____

4. a chair _____

5. a bed _____

6. shoes _____

7. a lamp _____

8. a hole _____

9. a child _____

10. a husband and wife _____

B. Read the paragraph. Write one word from the list on each line.

sound
~~beehives~~
honey
cakes
sweet

Bees are insects. They live in (1) _____beehives_____. They make a (2) _____ like "buzz, buzz, buzz." They also make a food called (3) _____. People buy the honey to put on bread or in (4) _____. They like the (5) _____ taste of honey.

Home, Sweet Home

One day, Mary VanSinclair heard a strange sound in her wall. She put her ear to the wall and listened. What did she hear? "Buzz, buzz, buzz."

Mary called her husband, Lorne. She told him there was something in the wall. Mary and Lorne made a big hole in the wall. Then they saw what was inside: bees! There was a big beehive in the wall, and there were hundreds of bees crawling around in there!

There was also lots of honey in the wall. At first, Mary and Lorne didn't know what to do. Then they decided to take the honey out. Lorne got a shovel and started to dig. He worked and worked, but the honey kept coming. Soon there was more than eight inches of honey on the floor!

Every day, Mary and Lorne took more honey out of their walls. Soon they had a big pail of honey—more than 50 pounds! Mary said, "There is honey everywhere. It's on our clothes and our furniture. It's even on my shoes. Now I'm three inches taller!" Mary and Lorne have decided to give their friends and relatives honey for Christmas.

Reading Skills

Read this paragraph. Find the answers to the questions below and underline them in the paragraph. Write the number of the question above the underlined words.

One day, Mary VanSinclair heard a strange sound in her wall. She

                                                                        1

put her ear to the wall and listened. She heard <u>"buzz, buzz, buzz."</u>

She called her husband, Lorne. She told him there was something

in the wall. Mary and Lorne made a big hole in the wall. Then

they saw what was inside: bees! There was a big beehive in the

wall, and there were hundreds of bees! There was also lots of

honey in the wall.

1. What sound did Mary VanSinclair hear in her wall?
2. What did she tell her husband?
3. What did Mary and Lorne do?
4. What did they see inside the wall?
5. How many bees were inside the wall?
6. What else did they see in the wall?

READING COMPREHENSION

Put the story in order. Write a number on each line.

_____   Lorne got a shovel and started to dig out the honey.

  1   Mary VanSinclair heard a buzzing sound in her wall.

_____   They saw hundreds of bees in the wall.

_____ Mary and Lorne made a hole in the wall.

_____ Mary and Lorne decided to give their friends honey for Christmas.

BUILD YOUR VOCABULARY

A. Read the sentences. Write one word from the list on each line.

honey
tall
bees
relatives
walls
~~shovel~~
pail

1. To dig in our garden, we use a ____shovel____.

2. People put _____ on toast or bread.

3. When we buy a new house, we will paint the _____ white.

4. In the summer, there are many _____ near flowers.

5. I carried water to my garden in a _____.

6. My uncles and aunts are in my family. They are my

_____.

7. My sister is 5'4" _____.

B. Write your own sentences using the words listed.

1. Honey is good to eat. _____

2. _____

3. _____

4. _____

5. _____

6. _____

7. _____

STUCK ON DUCT TAPE

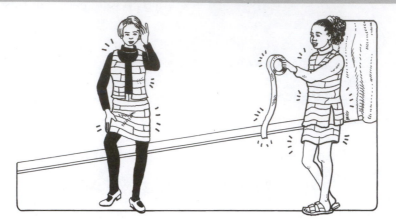

Before You Read

A. Look at the picture. Work with a partner. Talk about what you see.

B. What can you use to do each job? Work with a partner. Complete the chart.

	Glue	Tape	Thumbtack	Staple
1. put a picture on the wall		✓	✓	
2. put two pieces of paper together				
3. fix a hole in a boat				
4. close a bag of potato chips				
5. close an envelope				
6. fix a broken window				

Stuck on Duct Tape

What is duct tape? It's a kind of tape you can buy in a hardware store. It is silver on one side and sticky on the other side. It's not expensive, and it's very useful. People who fix things in their homes use it a lot. But now, suddenly, everyone is using it.

Duct tape is so popular that people have written books about it. There is also a radio show, a calendar, and some songs about duct tape. On the World Wide Web, there are many Web sites about duct tape. People have hundreds of ideas for how to use it.

How do people use duct tape? People who have a boat or canoe say it's great. If you have a small hole, you can put duct tape over it.

Then the water can't get inside. Many people used duct tape when there was a hurricane in Florida. One man said he put it around the doors of his house. The wind and rain were very strong, and the roof of his house came off. But the doors stayed on!

People don't use duct tape just to repair things. Some teenage girls used it to make skirts, tops, and sandals for a fashion show at their high school. Everyone loved their new clothes. "They're different. They're so shiny," one girl said. Other people use duct tape to keep potato chip bags closed or to hold their wallets together. "It's great," one man says. "This silver tape is part of our culture!"

Reading Skills

READ FOR THE MAIN IDEA

Reread the story. What is it about? Circle the letter of the correct answer.

a. Duct tape is good for repairing boats.

b. Duct tape is not expensive.

c. People everywhere use duct tape for all kinds of things.

REVIEW THE VOCABULARY

Read the list of information about duct tape. Complete the chart.

	Description	Use
1. repair boats		✓
2. make sandals		
3. fix things in the house		
4. shiny		
5. silver		
6. hold a wallet together		
7. put on a door in a hurricane		
8. sticky		
9. not expensive		
10. fix clothes		
11. useful		
12. close potato chip bags		

BUILD YOUR VOCABULARY

Look at these pairs of words. Write S if they mean the same thing.
Write D if they mean different things.

1. inexpensive   cheap   S

2. roof   door   ____

3. fix   repair _____

4. outfit   clothes _____

5. stick things together   hold things together _____

6. sticky   silver _____

Put It Together

Read the paragraph. Write one word from the list on each line.

basement	We all need to (1) _____fix_____ things in our (2) _____.
~~fix~~	Some problems such as (3) _____ in the wall need to
tape	be fixed. Problems such as water in the (4) _____
wallet	need pails. If air comes in near a window, we can use duct
holes	(5) _____ to stop it. This special (6)_____-colored
homes	tape can also fix a hole in your (7) _____. Many people
duct	say (8) _____ tape is great!
silver	

TELL THE STORIES

A. Tell the story "Home, Sweet Home" to another student in the class. First draw pictures of the story. Then use the pictures to help you tell the story. Use these questions to help you remember information, but tell the story in your own words.

1. What did Mr. and Mrs. VanSinclair hear in the wall?

2. What did they see when they made a hole in the wall?

3. How did they take the honey out?

4. What did they do with the honey?

B. Tell the story "Stuck on Duct Tape" to your teacher or to another student in the class. Talk about these things.

1. what duct tape looks like
2. five ways to use duct tape

Add three other ways to use duct tape.

TALK ABOUT IT

Work in groups to discuss the ideas below.

1. Make a list of some problems people can have with their houses.
2. Discuss ways to solve these problems. Talk about whom you can call or what you can do.

SOLVE THE PROBLEM

Discuss these situations in groups. Talk about things to do or say.

1. You just moved into a new apartment and find some insects in the kitchen and bathroom.
2. It is cold outside, and air is coming in around your window.

IN YOUR NEIGHBORHOOD

What kinds of tools do people usually have in their homes? What are they for? Look at this list of tools and things in the house. Ask one or two neighbors if they have these things and how they use them.

a hammer	a pail
pliers	a tape measure
duct tape	a shovel
a saw	

Seeing Double

STORY 1   THE TWINS DAY FESTIVAL

STORY 2   TWO PLUS TWO

Let's Get Ready

Work with a partner. Read these questions. Write the letter of the correct answer on the line.

1. Which word means *exactly the same*? __d__

2. Which word goes with *husband*? ____

3. What is a room in the house? ____

4. What is a *carpenter*? ____

5. What do many people wear? ____

6. What is the opposite of *child*? ____

7. What do people watch? ____

8. What do you use to speak? ____

a. bathroom
b. television
c. a worker
d. identical
e. your voice
f. adult
g. wife
h. jeans and T-shirts

Before You Read

A. Read the paragraph. Write one word from the list on each line.

mother

same

wife

~~babies~~

sisters

identical

sound

Twins are two (1) ___babies___ that are born at the same time to the same (2) _____. They can be two brothers, two (3) _____, or a brother and a sister. Only two brothers or two sisters can be (4) _____ twins. Identical twins look exactly the (5) _____. Often they even (6) _____ the same when they talk. Sometimes even their mother and father, or their husband or (7) _____, can't tell one twin from the other.

B. What do you know about twins? Work with a partner. Read the sentences. Write **T** *for* **true** *or* **F** *for* **false.**

1. It is easy for twins to find husbands and wives. _____

2. Many twins get divorced. _____

3. Twins like to do things together. _____

4. A person who marries a twin often feels lonely. _____

5. Many twins never marry. _____

C. Scan the story to check your answers.

The Twins Day Festival

If you visit Twinsburg, Ohio, in August, you will think that you are seeing double. This is where the Twins Day Festival takes place. It is the biggest gathering of twins in the world. Every year, about 2,500 to 3,000 sets of identical twins come to the festival. There are little babies, children, teenagers, and adults. There are even twins who are over 90 years old.

The Twins Day Festival is like one big party. People meet old friends and make new friends.

There are competitions to see which twins look the most alike and which twins look the least alike. People eat hot dogs, play games, and take pictures together.

Some twins go to the festival hoping to find love. Finding someone to love is difficult for twins, because twins are very close. "Being a twin is very special," one twin said. "It's hard for a non-twin to understand this special relationship." Non-twins who marry twins often feel lonely and left out. Many twins and non-twins who marry get divorced. Many twins never marry because they are so happy with their twins.

At the Twins Day Festival, some twins are lucky and find love. Doug and Phil Malm met their wives, Jill and Jena, at the festival. Doug explains how it happened. "We first met Jena and Jill on Friday night. Then we met them again several times on the weekend." The two sets of twins fell in love, and Doug and Phil asked Jill and Jena to marry them. Doug and Phil thought they asked, "Will you marry me?" What they really said was, "Will you marry us?"

Reading Skills

READING COMPREHENSION

Reread the story and answer the questions. Write the answers on the lines.

1. Where is the Twins Day Festival? _____Twinsburg, Ohio_____

2. How many people go to the Twins Day Festival? _____

   _____

3. What are the ages of the people who go to the festival? _____

   _____

4. Name three things people do at the festival. _____

   _____

5. What do some twins want to find at the festival? _____

6. Why is finding love difficult for twins? _____

   _____

7. What often happens when twins marry non-twins? _____

   _____

8. Which four people met and fell in love at the festival? _____

   _____

9. What did Doug and Phil ask Jill and Jena? _____

   _____

BUILD YOUR VOCABULARY

Read each sentence below. Look at the underlined word or words. Circle the letter of the word or words that mean the same.

1. You will think that you are <u>seeing double.</u>

   (a.) seeing two things that are the same

   b. seeing a lot of different things

2. It is the biggest <u>gathering</u> of twins in the world.

   a. group of people

   b. place to go

3. Every year, about 2,500 to 3,000 sets of <u>identical</u> twins come to the festival.

   a. twins that are brother and sister

   b. twins that look exactly the same

4. There are babies, children, <u>teenagers</u>, and adults.

   a. people younger than 12 years old

   b. people between 13 and 19 years old

5. Twins are very <u>close</u>.

   a. have the same feelings and ideas

   b. stand together all the time

TWO PLUS TWO

Before You Read

~~night~~

TV

T-shirts

carpenter

~~morning~~

jeans

stereo

daycare
worker

washing
clothes

dusting
furniture

A. Look at the picture. Work with a partner. Talk about what you see.

B. Look at the categories below. Complete the chart.

	night	morning
1. times of day	night	morning
2. kinds of jobs		
3. chores		
4. clothes		
5. kinds of entertainment		

Two Plus Two

Sometimes Phil Malm is not sure which woman is his wife. If his wife, Jena, is sleeping on the couch next to her sister, Jill, Phil says, "Sweetheart?" to see who answers. This is because Jena and Jill are identical twins. They look exactly the same.

Jill and Jena look alike, and they also do the same things. They speak at the same time, and their voices sound the same. "When we were young, we always got one of everything. We got one TV, one car, one stereo. It was like we were one person," says Jill. Even now as adults, they do almost everything together. Some mornings, Jill says, "What are we wearing today?" and Jena answers, "We're wearing jeans and T-shirts."

Jill is married to Doug Malm, and Jena is married to Phil Malm.

Doug and Phil are also identical twins. Jill and Doug live in the same house as Phil and Jena. They say they are very happy living together. "If we have a problem, we stay up all night to talk about it," says Jena.

"We do all our chores together," the twins explain. Jill and Jena do the cooking together. One twin dusts the furniture, and the other twin cleans the bathrooms. When they wash clothes, Jena does the dark colors, and Jill does the whites.

Jill and Jena love children, and they both work as daycare teachers. Doug and Phil work together, too. They have a carpentry business in Moscow, Idaho. "At work, we don't have a routine," says Doug. "Every day, we see what there is to do. If one of us doesn't want to do a job, we try to get our twin to do it!"

Reading Skills

Read the sentences. Write **T** *for* **true** *or* **F** *for* **false**. *Correct the wrong information.*

1. Jill and Jena look different. <u>F   the same</u>

2. Jill and Jena's voices sound the same. _____

3. When Jill and Jena were young, they had their own TVs.

   _____

4. Jill and Jena wear the same kind of clothes. _____

5. Phil and Doug are married to Jill and Jena. _____

6. Phil and Doug are also identical twins. _____

7. The twins have a lot of problems living together. _____

8. Doug and Jena usually clean the house together. _____

9. Jill and Jena work in a children's hospital. _____

10. Doug and Phil have a business together. _____

BUILD YOUR VOCABULARY

Cross out the word in each group that doesn't belong.

1. identical   alike   the same   ~~different~~
2. car   TV   happy   stereo
3. speak   together   talk   answer
4. morning   dust   wash   clean
5. wife   sister   jeans   husband
6. work   job   chores   married
7. day   morning   twin   night
8. jeans   clothes   cooking   T-shirts

REVIEW THE VOCABULARY

Complete each group of words. Write one word from the list on each line.

look
sleep
dust
wear
clean
live
~~stay up~~
cook

1. ___stay up___ all night
2. _____ the furniture
3. _____ on a couch
4. _____ alike
5. _____ food
6. _____ the bathroom
7. _____ jeans
8. _____ together

Put It Together

A. Use the words below to complete the crossword puzzle. Read the stories again to help you.

Festival
~~brothers~~
together
house
same
two
twins
identical
clean
wife
sisters

Across

4. Identical twins can be two sisters or two ___brothers___.

5. Jena and Jill are twin _____.

8. Twins that look exactly alike are called _____ twins.

9. Sometimes it is hard for a male twin to find a _____.

10. Twins go to the Twins Day _____ in Twinsburg, Ohio.

Down

1. Twins often do many things _____.

2. Jill and Doug Malm live in the same _____ as Jena and Phil Malm.

3. Twins are _____ babies that are born at the same time to the same mother.

5. Twins usually look and act the _____.

6. Phil and Doug Malm are identical _____.

7. Jena and Jill like to _____ the house together.

B. Find the opposites. Write one word from the list on each line.

divorce	1. most _____least_____
smallest	2. alike _____
different	3. twin _____
sister	4. brother _____
unlucky	5. old _____
single	6. marry _____
~~least~~	7. lucky _____
non-twin	8. biggest_____
new	9. children_____
adults	10. double_____

TELL THE STORIES

A. Tell the story "The Twins Day Festival" to another student in the class. Choose four facts that are true from the story. Add one fact that is not true. See if your partner can tell which fact is false.

B. Tell the story "Two Plus Two" to a small group in the class. Imagine that you are the mother or father of twins or that you have a twin brother or sister. Explain what is easy and difficult about being a twin. Describe what the twins do together and how people tell which twin is which. Use the information from the story to help you.

TALK ABOUT IT

Discuss these questions in groups.

1. Do you know any twins? How do they act together?
2. Would you like to have a twin? Why or why not?
3. Do you think twins should be dressed the same way? Why or why not?

SOLVE THE PROBLEM

Discuss these situations in groups. Talk about things to do or say.

1. The sisters and brothers in your family fight all the time.
2. Your sisters or brothers are much older than you and are very close. You feel left out.
3. You become friends with a set of twins. Sometimes you can't tell them apart.
4. A family friend is expecting a baby. She finds out she will have twins.

IN YOUR NEIGHBORHOOD

Are there any twins living in your community? What are their names and ages? If possible, tell them about the Twins Day Festival. Do they think it's a good idea?

WRITING OPTION

Is it fun to be a twin? Write a paragraph telling some good things and some bad things about being a twin.

Working Overtime

STORY 1   HELP ON WHEELS

STORY 2   THE SINGING DOCTOR

Let's Get Ready

A. Where do people work? Match each List A item with a List B item.

List A

1. on the road _g_

2. in a hospital ____

3. on television ____

4. in a garage ____

5. in a school ____

6. on a farm ____

7. in a store ____

8. in an office ____

9. in an airplane ____

10. in a restaurant ____

List B

a. cook

b. teacher

c. secretary

d. farmer

e. entertainer

f. doctor

g. tow truck driver

h. flight attendant

i. salesclerk

j. mechanic

B. Work in groups. Make a list of all the jobs you can think of. Write your lists on the board. Then compare your lists. Which jobs do many groups have on their lists? Which jobs do only one or two groups have on their lists?

Before You Read

Look at the picture of the woman driving a tow truck. Discuss these questions in groups.

1. Did you ever call a tow truck for your car?
2. What was the problem with your car?
3. What did the tow truck driver do?

Help on Wheels

Jenny Woznuk and her husband, Philip Briere, are sometimes on the road for 14 hours. The weather is often cold, and the roads are icy, but they don't complain. "It's great," Jenny says. "We work very hard, but we love this job. We're doing what we want to do."

What is Jenny's job? She drives a tow truck. Not many women drive tow trucks. It's hard work, and you have to be strong. Sometimes people are surprised to see Jenny drive up in her truck. They think a woman can't do the job. But when they see Jenny work, they are not surprised anymore. They are just happy that Jenny can help them.

Jenny and her husband started their own towing company four years ago. They tow cars that break down or are in accidents. Jenny drives a tow truck and works in the office. Her husband also drives a tow truck and does repairs. Now many people know Jenny. "I have a lot of good customers," she says. "I think it's because I really want to help people. When you go to an accident, you have to help people with their cars. But you also have to talk to the people. Sometimes they are very upset or they are hurt. I really enjoy what I'm doing. I guess I do it well."

How did Jenny decide to start driving a tow truck? "I liked cars. My father worked with cars, and I always helped him," she says. "My husband is a mechanic. One day, we decided to start our own company." What does Jenny do to relax after work? "I fix cars!" she says.

Reading Skills

READING COMPREHENSION

Read each question. Circle the letter of the correct answer.

1. Why is Jenny on the road for 14 hours?
   a. She travels to other cities.
   b. Her job is to drive a tow truck.

2. Why are people surprised to see Jenny drive up in her tow truck?

    a. Not many women drive tow trucks.

    b. Jenny is too young to drive a tow truck.

3. Which jobs does Jenny do?

    a. She drives a tow truck and does repairs.

    b. She drives a tow truck and works in the office.

4. Why does Jenny like her job?

    a. She likes to help people when they are upset or hurt.

    b. She likes to drive a big truck.

5. How did Jenny get interested in cars?

    a. She helped her father fix cars.

    b. She took a course to become a car mechanic.

6. What does Jenny do for fun?

    a. She watches TV shows about cars.

    b. She fixes cars.

BUILD YOUR VOCABULARY

One word in each group doesn't belong. Cross out that word.

Group A	Group B	Group C	Group D
accident	cold	truck	fix
hurt	work	mechanic	repair
upset	weather	relax	customer
~~happy~~	icy	car	tow

BUILD YOUR VOCABULARY

A. Reread the story. To complete the paragraph, write one word from the story on each line.

Jenny Woznuk sometimes drives a tow (1) ____truck____ for

14 hours. The weather is often (2) _____. Not many

(3) _____ drive tow trucks. It is hard work, and you have

to be (4) _____ . But Jenny loves her (5) _____.

She likes to help (6) _____ . She works with her

(7) _____ . He drives a tow truck and (8) _____ cars.

B. Write your own sentences using the words you used above.

1. _____

2. _____

3. _____

4. _____

5. _____

6. _____

7. _____

8. _____

GIVE YOUR OPINION

What do you think? Discuss these questions in groups.

1. Is it unusual for a woman to drive a tow truck?

2. Do you think a woman has more problems driving a tow truck than a man? Explain why or why not.

3. What are other jobs that you have to be physically strong to do?

Before You Read

Some of these words are about doctors. Some are about singers.
Complete the chart.

	Doctor	Singer
1. sings a song		✓
2. takes care of patients		
3. explains a medical problem		
4. sings on TV		
5. helps sick people		
6. writes love songs		
7. works in a hospital		
8. performs in Las Vegas		
9. gives medical advice		
10. went to medical school		

The Singing Doctor

Nick Petrella is a doctor in Montreal. He works 60 hours a week. He takes care of 150 patients a week in the hospital and at his office. He's been a doctor for ten years.

Dr. Petrella gives his patients good medical advice. But he doesn't just tell his patients what to do. He also sings to them on television! Dr. Petrella has his own TV show. The show is in Italian, English, and French. The doctor starts the show with a song and then gives medical advice. He explains a medical problem or disease in simple language. After that, he sings another song.

Dr. Petrella produces and performs in his own show every week. The program is very popular with his patients and with people who enjoy his singing. His dream is to perform in Las Vegas. His favorite songs are love songs, and he has a compact disk of love songs that he wrote. Dr. Petrella says, "I always loved to sing. All my problems are gone when I sing." But when Dr. Petrella was young, his father didn't want him to be a singer. So he went to medical school.

Some people tell Dr. Petrella he can help people more as a doctor. But Dr. Petrella says he helps people when he sings, too. "I like to make people smile. Sometimes it's difficult to make a sick person smile. Medicine and entertainment both try to do the same thing. They try to make people feel good."

Reading Skills

Read each sentence below. Circle the letter of the correct answer.

1. Dr. Petrella works
   a. a few hours a week.
   b. many hours a week.

2. Dr. Petrella is special because he
   a. gives medical advice.
   b. sings on television.

3. Dr. Petrella's show is
   a. in two languages.
   b. in three languages.

4. In his TV show, Dr. Petrella
   a. sings and gives medical advice.
   b. sings about different diseases.

5. Dr. Petrella's show is
   a. popular in Las Vegas.
   b. popular with his patients.

6. Dr. Petrella
   a. made a compact disk of his own songs.
   b. bought a compact disk with love songs.

7. Nick Petrella went to medical school because
   a. his father didn't want him to be a singer.
   b. his father didn't want him to be a doctor.

8. Dr. Petrella says he like to
   a. help people sing.
   b. make people smile.

BUILD YOUR VOCABULARY

Read the paragraph. Write one word from the list on each line.

good
sing
~~hospital~~
songs
show
patients
medical
smile

Dr. Petrella works in a (1) ___hospital___. Every week he takes care of 150 (2) _____. On the weekend, Dr. Petrella has his own television (3) _____. He sings (4) _____, and then he gives (5) _____ advice to his patients. Dr. Petrella says he loves to (6) _____. He likes to make people (7) _____. He says that medicine and entertainment try to do the same thing. They try to make people feel (8) _____.

REVIEW THE VOCABULARY

Match each List A item with a List B item.

List A

1. sing
2. give
3. make
4. work
5. take care of

List B

a. 60 hours a week
b. a song
c. patients
d. advice
e. people smile

Put It Together

Here are some words from the stories. The letters are in the wrong order. Put the letters in the correct order. Use the information to help you.

1. otw _____tow_____   a way to pull cars

2. otrdoc _____   a person who helps sick people

3. itsopahl _____   a place where sick people go

4. droa _____   a place you drive

5. dentccia _____   when one car hits another car

6. gons _____   something you sing

7. imsle _____   something you do when you are happy

8. owsh _____   something you watch on TV

9. canichme _____   a person who fixes cars

10. aptinet _____   a sick person in a hospital

TELL THE STORIES

A. Tell the story "Help on Wheels" to a small group in the class. Imagine that you are driving and your car breaks down. You call a tow truck. Jenny Woznuk arrives to help you. You are surprised to see a woman driving a tow truck, and you ask Jenny about her work.

Tell your group how Jenny helped you and how you felt. Explain what Jenny told you about her job. Use the information from the story to help you.

B. Tell the story "The Singing Doctor" to a small group in the class. Imagine that you go to the emergency room of a hospital and Dr. Petrella helps you. The next day, you turn on the television and see Dr. Petrella singing and giving medical advice.

Explain how Dr. Petrella helped you and about his TV show. After class, tell this story to a friend or a student in another class.

TALK ABOUT IT

Discuss these questions in groups.

1. What is the best job you ever had?
2. What is the worst job you ever had?
3. Did you ever have an unusual job? What was it?
4. Do you think there are some jobs that are men's jobs or women's jobs? What are they?

SOLVE THE PROBLEM

Discuss these situations in groups. Talk about things to do or say.

1. You apply for a job. The interviewer tells you that this job is only for a man (you are a woman) or only for a woman (you are a man). You think you can do the job, and you want it.
2. You are in the emergency room of a hospital. You prefer a doctor of the same gender as you. A doctor of the other gender comes to examine you.

WRITING OPTION

A. Write a note to Jenny Woznuk. Imagine that your car broke down and Jenny came to help you. Thank her for helping you.

B. Write a letter to Dr. Petrella. Say why you like his show.

Two Chewy Tales

STORY 1   WATCH OUT FOR THE DOLL!

STORY 2   A CHEWY SUBJECT

Let's Get Ready

A. What are these things? Match the words to the pictures.

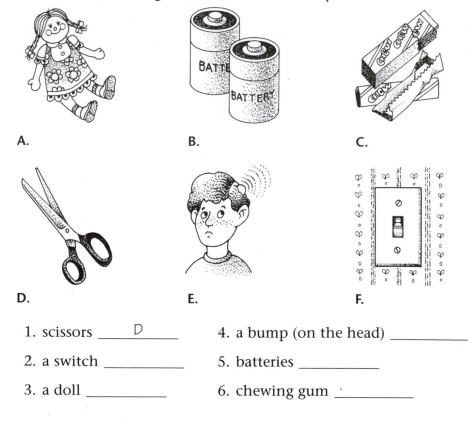

A.

B.

C.

D.

E.

F.

1. scissors _____D_____

2. a switch _____

3. a doll _____

4. a bump (on the head) _____

5. batteries _____

6. chewing gum _____

B. Work with a partner. Look at the pictures. Talk about the problems you see.

A.

B.

C.

Before You Read

Work with a partner. Look at the pictures. Talk about what you see. What do you think this story is about?

Watch Out for the Doll!

The day after Christmas, Sharon Kenton took her five-year-old daughter Cindy to daycare. At two o'clock, she heard the telephone ring. It was Cindy's daycare teacher. The teacher told Mrs. Kenton to come to the daycare center quickly. A doll was eating Cindy's hair!

When Mrs. Kenton got to the daycare center, she saw Cindy holding the doll and screaming. The teacher explained that Cindy was taking a nap with her new doll beside her. Suddenly, Cindy felt the doll chewing her hair and started to scream. Mrs. Kenton said, "It looked really bad. The doll chewed Cindy's long hair all the way to her head." She rushed Cindy to a doctor, who cut off Cindy's hair with scissors. Cindy had a big bump on her head.

The doll was a new toy that eats plastic food. When there is some-thing in the doll's mouth, it begins to chew. The problem is that there is no switch to stop the doll from chewing. There are batteries in the doll, but it is hard to take them out.

The doll was a popular Christmas gift. The day after Christmas, five children had problems with the doll. Each time, it was the same. The doll began to eat the child's hair, and the parents couldn't shut the doll off. One mother said, "The doll pulled out my little girl's hair from the roots! She has a bald spot on the back of her head!"

Some people returned their dolls to the store. They wanted their money back. But Cindy still loves her doll. "We're going to keep the doll," Mrs. Kenton said, "but we took the batteries out."

Reading Skills

READING COMPREHENSION

One word or phrase in each sentence is not correct. Cross out the incorrect word or words. Write the correct word or words on each line.

1. Five-year-old Cindy was at ~~school~~. _____ *daycare* _____

2. The teacher called Cindy's sister. _____

3. Cindy laughed because the doll was eating her hair. _____

   _____

4. Cindy's teacher took her to the doctor. _____

5. The doctor cut off Cindy's hair with a knife. _____

6. Cindy had a bump on her hand. _____

7. The doll eats real food. _____

8. It is easy to take the batteries out of the doll. _____

9. Many children got this kind of doll as a birthday gift. _____

   _____

10. Two other children had problems with the doll. _____

11. Some people returned their dolls to the daycare center. _____

    _____

12. Cindy returned her doll. _____

BUILD YOUR VOCABULARY

Read each sentence below. Look at the underlined words. Circle the letter of the words that mean the same.

1. Five-year-old Cindy was <u>taking a nap.</u>
   a. playing
   b. sleeping

2. Cindy began to <u>scream</u>.
   a. cry
   b. make a loud noise

3. A doll was <u>chewing</u> Cindy's hair.
   a. eating
   b. touching

4. Cindy had a big <u>bump</u> on her head.

    a. cut

    b. bruise

5. The parents couldn't <u>shut the doll off</u>.

    a. put the doll on the floor

    b. stop the doll's chewing

6. Some people <u>returned their dolls to the store</u>.

    a. brought them back to the store

    b. bought new dolls at the store

UNDERSTAND THE PRONOUNS

Look at each underlined word. Write a word from the list that matches the underlined word.

the teacher
~~Cindy~~
the doll
the children's
Mrs. Kenton
some people
the batteries

1. <u>She</u> put her head down on the table. _____Cindy_____

2. <u>She</u> said, "A doll is chewing Cindy's hair." _____

3. <u>She</u> rushed Cindy to a doctor. _____

4. <u>It</u> eats plastic food. _____

5. The dolls began to eat <u>their</u> hair. _____

6. There are batteries in the doll, but it is hard to take <u>them</u> out.

_____

7. <u>They</u> wanted their money back. _____

Before You Read

A. What do you know about chewing gum? Work with a partner. Read the sentences. Write **T** *for* **true** *or* **F** *for* **false.**

1. People started chewing gum about 50 years ago. __F__

2. Wrigley's gum is very popular in America. ____

3. Children under ten years old chew the most gum. ____

4. People in Utah chew the most gum. ____

5. Americans chew 90,000 tons of gum every year. ____

6. People who work in schools take gum off chairs and tables

   every day. ____

B. Scan the story to check if your answers are correct. Underline the correct information in the story.

A Chewy Subject

What do children love and teachers hate? Chewing gum. People who work in schools say it takes half an hour every day to take the gum off chairs and tables.

People have chewed gum for a long time. Scientists in Sweden found a piece of chewing gum that is 9,000 years old. It had the tooth marks of a teenager on it! But modern chewing gum was first made around 1870. Thomas Adams, an inventor, got some liquid from a tree in Mexico. He wanted to make rubber, but instead he found a way to make chewing gum.

Adams's gum was a big success, and soon other people began to make gum. In 1892, William Wrigley Jr., started to make gum. He sent pieces of gum to everyone listed in the U.S. phone books. People began to chew his gum, and he became one of the richest people in the United States. Today the Wrigley company makes 1 billion sticks of gum a year!

Americans chew more than 90,000 tons of gum every year. Teenagers between 12 and 14 years old chew about 40 percent of the gum made every year. And people in Utah chew more gum than people in other states. Some people aren't happy about this much gum. People who worked at the Statue of Liberty thought there was too much gum to clean up, so they put in a trash can. The trash can had a sign over it. It said, "Put your gum here." Many people put their gum on the sign!

Reading Skills

UNDERSTAND THE DETAILS

What do these numbers mean? Write the letter of the correct answer on the line.

1. 1870 __d__

2. 90,000 ____

3. 12–14 year olds ____

4. 9,000 years old ____

5. 1892 ____

6. 1 billion ____

7. half an hour each day ____

a. the year William Wrigley Jr., started to make gum

b. the people who chew 40 percent of the gum made every year

c. the number of tons of gum Americans chew every year

d. the year modern chewing gum was invented

e. the age of a piece of chewing gum

f. the number of sticks of gum the Wrigley company makes each year

g. the time it takes to take gum off chairs and tables in schools

SCAN FOR THE DETAILS

Find this information in the story. Write the answers on the lines.

1. two people who made chewing gum ___Thomas Adams___

   William Wrigley Jr. _____

2. a person who hates chewing gum _____

3. a country where people found an old piece of chewing gum

   _____

4. what Thomas Adams wanted to make _____

5. people Wrigley sent gum to _____

_____

6. the state where people chew the most gum _____

7. why workers at the Statue of Liberty put in a trash can _____

_____

8. the words on the sign at the Statue of Liberty _____

_____

9. the place where people put their gum _____

BUILD YOUR VOCABULARY

A. Read the sentences. Write a word or words from the list on each line.

phone
book

trash can

rich

tooth

liquids

success

modern

rubber

1. Mr. and Mrs. Smith have a lot of money. They are very

_____rich_____.

2. Alice ate this apple. It has her _____ marks on it.

3. Margaret does her job very well. She is a _____.

4. Please put your garbage in the _____ near the door.

5. I didn't know your number, so I looked it up in the

_____.

6. Car tires are made of _____.

7. Water and juice are kinds of _____.

8. Our school is not old. It is new and _____.

B. Write your own sentences using the words listed.

1. _____

2. _____

3. _____

4. _____

5. _____

6. _____

7. _____

8. _____

Put It Together

Which items belong in each group? Put a check mark (✓) beside the words that belong.

8 Things in the House	8 Places	8 Days, Dates, or Times
✓ chair	____ Utah	____ Christmas
____ table	____ daycare center	____ every day
____ scissors	____ teacher	____ 1870
____ car tires	____ Sweden	____ pull
____ batteries	____ Mexico	____ 9,000 years ago
____ tree	____ difficult	____ inventor
____ phone book	____ school	____ the day after Christmas
____ table	____ United States	____ half an hour
____ school	____ Statue of Liberty	____ 1892
____ trash can	____ gum	____ today
____ plastic cups	____ store	____ ton

TELL THE STORIES

A. Work in groups to act out the story "Watch Out for the Doll!" You need the following actors:

Cindy

Mrs. Kenton

a daycare teacher

a doctor

a storyteller

Practice what you will say and do. Then act out the story for the class. The storyteller explains the problem with the doll and what people can do if they have this kind of doll.

B. Tell the story "A Chewy Subject" to another student in the class. Choose four facts that are true from the story. Add one fact that is not true. See if your partner can tell which fact is false.

TALK ABOUT IT

Discuss these questions in groups.

1. Do you like to chew gum? Why or why not?
2. How often do you chew gum?
3. What kind of gum do you like?
4. Should children be allowed to chew gum in school?
5. In which places is it not a good idea to chew gum?
6. Did you ever step on gum in the street? What did you do?
7. What is a polite way to get rid of gum?

SOLVE THE PROBLEM

Discuss these situations in groups. Talk about things to do or say.

1. You buy a toy for your niece. The first time she plays with it, the toy breaks.

2. You buy a toy for a child in your family. The batteries run out very quickly. The child asks you to buy new batteries every week.

3. A child in your family wants a new toy that he or she sees on television. You don't think this is a good toy. It is expensive, and it breaks quickly.

IN YOUR NEIGHBORHOOD

Go to a store in your neighborhood that sells gum. Find this information.

1. Write the names of three different kinds of gum.

   _____   _____   _____

2. Write three flavors of gum that you see.

   _____   _____   _____

3. Write the name and price of one kind of gum. _____

4. Write the name of one kind of mint gum. _____

5. Write the name of one kind of fruit gum. _____

6. Write the name of one kind of bubble gum. _____

WRITING OPTION

Write a memo asking students not to chew gum in your school. Explain why.

ANSWER KEY

Unit 1   Pennies from Heaven

Let's Get Ready   *Page 1*

2. quarters   4. checks
3. dollars   5. credit

STORY 1   A GIFT FROM AN ANGEL

Before You Read   *Page 2*

B.

2. A   3. D   4. B

Reading Skills

READING COMPREHENSION   *Page 3*

2. ~~man~~   woman   5. ~~bill~~   check
3. ~~address~~   name   6. ~~nobody~~   anyone
4. ~~Texas~~   California   7. ~~$2,000~~ $2 million

BUILD YOUR VOCABULARY   *Page 4*

2. check   4. furniture   6. family
3. name   5. money

REVIEW THE INFORMATION   *Page 5*

2. Dora   5. Angel   8. Dora
3. Dora   6. Angel   9. Dora
4. Dora   7. Dora   10. Dora

STORY 2   MONEY FROM THE SKY

Before You Read   *Page 6*

2. F   4. T
3. T   5. F

Reading Skills

READING COMPREHENSION   *Page 7*

2. b   4. b   6. b
3. b   5. a

BUILD YOUR VOCABULARY   *Page 8*

Paragraph B: neighborhood, return
Paragraph C: are poor, food
Paragraph D: drawers, back yard, steal
Paragraph E: firefighter

CHOOSE A TITLE   *Page 9*

b

Put It Together

LET'S REVIEW

A.   *Page 10*

Across	Down
4. flood	1. Angel
7. poor	2. hundred
8. check	4. furniture
9. crime	5. money
10. help	6. truck

B.   *Page 12*

3. person   8. thing   13. person
4. action   9. action   14. place
5. thing   10. place   15. person
6. action   11. person   16. action
7. person   12. thing

Unit 2   Little Heroes

Let's Get Ready   *Page 15*

2. c   4. b   6. c
3. a   5. a

STORY 1   SAVE MY MOM!

Before You Read   *Page 16*

2. a   3. b

Reading Skills

READ FOR THE MAIN IDEA   *Page 17*

c

READING COMPREHENSION   *Page 18*

2, 5, 1, 4, 3, 6

GIVE THE REASONS   *Page 18*

2. e   4. b
3. d   5. a

REVIEW THE VOCABULARY   *Page 19*

A.
2. kitchen   5. firefighter   8. address
3. dentist   6. operator
4. voice   7. ambulance

STORY 2   MY BROTHER'S IN THE DRYER!

Before You Read   *Page 20*

C, A, D, B

Reading Skills

READ FOR THE MAIN IDEA   *Page 22*

b

2. 4
3. at the baby sitter's house
4. screams from the clothes dryer
5. hide-and-seek
6. to hide
7. another child
8. It was broken.
9. He didn't let go.
10. He pulled David out.
11. They were broken.
12. a superhero
13. He couldn't stop it.

USE THE INFORMATION *Page 23*

2. Dustin
3. the baby sitter
4. Dustin, David, and another child
5. Dustin
6. David
7. David
8. Dustin

Put It Together

LET'S REVIEW *Page 23*

2. S	6. D	9. D	12. S
3. D	7. D	10. S	13. S
4. S	8. D	11. D	14. D
5. S			

B. *Page 24*

2. g	4. e	6. c	8. b
3. f	5. d	7. a	

Unit 3   Winning the Contest

Let's Get Ready   *Page 27*

2. a	5. h	8. b
3. e	6. j	9. i
4. d	7. c	10. g

STORY 1   COURIERS IN THE COLD

Before You Read   *Page 28*

A.
2. a   5. c
3. e   6. b
4. f

B.
2. T   4. F
3. F   5. T

Reading Skills

READING COMPREHENSION   *Page 30*

2. They drive trucks.
3. uniforms
4. The couriers had to wear shorts and short socks. They could not wear pants, long socks, or sweaters.
5. six
6. minus 30 degrees
7. The couriers were in short pants.
8. short pants

BUILD YOUR VOCABULARY   *Page 31*

A.
2. G   5. H   7. A
3. C   6. F   8. D
4. E

B.

Summer	Winter
shirts	jackets
short socks	gloves
	sweaters
	long socks

STORY 2   THE BIGGEST PUMPKIN

Before You Read   *Page 32*

2. b   4. b   6. c
3. c   5. c

Reading Skills

READING COMPREHENSION   *Page 34*

2. T   4. F   6. F   8. T
3. F   5. T   7. F

BUILD YOUR VOCABULARY   *Page 34*

Fruits	Vegetables
1. watermelon	pumpkin
2. melon	squash
3. cantaloupe	cabbage
4. pineapple	zucchini
5. strawberry	radish
6. lemon	cucumber
7. tomato	carrot
8. grapefruit	onion
9. apple	potato

MAKE COMPARISONS   *Page 35*

2. bigger   5. smaller   8. smaller
3. smaller   6. smaller   9. smaller
4. smaller   7. bigger   10. bigger

Put It Together

LET'S REVIEW   *Page 36*

2. d   6. f
3. e   7. a
4. c   8. h
5. g

Unit 4   Animal Encounters

Let's Get Ready   *Page 40*

A.

2. E	4. D	6. A
3. B	5. F	

B. *Page 41*

2. cats, birds, dogs, fish
3. alligators, fish
4. birds, alligators, fish
5. cats, birds, alligators, dogs
6. birds
7. alligators (some kinds of dogs)
8. cats, birds, alligators, dogs, fish
9. cats, birds, dogs, fish
10. fish (some kinds of birds such as chickens; alligators, cats, or dogs in some places)

Note: Other answers may be possible.

| STORY 1   THE ENGINE THAT PURRED |

Reading Skills

READING COMPREHENSION   *Page 43*

A.

Things that are true:
1, 3, 7, 8

B.

4, 1, 5, 2, 3, 6

REVIEW THE VOCABULARY   *Page 45*

Car: surprise
Cat: garage
People: scared
Feelings: engine

2. rats or birds
3. the cat
4. the car owner

5. the people in the garage
6. the cat's owner

STORY 2   ALLIGATOR ATTACK!

Reading Skills

READING COMPREHENSION   *Page 47*

2. her son, her friend Susie, and Susie's young daughters
3. It was very safe.
4. a noise and a louder sound (a splash)
5. an alligator
6. huge, as big as the canoe
7. when it turned over in the water
8. Everyone was afraid.
9. She grabbed the paddle and rowed to shore.
10. They don't hurt you if you don't hurt them.
11. She hit it on the head with the paddle.

READING COMPREHENSION   *Page 48*

2. 1, 2
3. 2, 1

4. 1, 2
5. 2, 1

6. 2, 1

REVIEW THE VOCABULARY   *Page 49*

2. alligator
3. alligator
4. Loretta
5. park people
6. park people

7. alligator
8. Loretta
9. Loretta
10. Loretta

Put It Together

LET'S REVIEW *Page 50*

A.
2. engine	6. neighbor's
3. surprised	7. garage
4. alive	8. milk
5. owner	

B.
2. camping	6. hand
3. safe	7. afraid
4. Splash	8. hurt
5. alligator	

Unit 5   A Helping Hand

Let's Get Ready   *Page 53*

2. g	6. c
3. d	7. f
4. a	8. b
5. e	

STORY 1   THE TEDDY BEAR LADY

Before You Read   *Page 54*

2. a   3. a

Reading Skills

READ FOR THE MAIN IDEA   *Page 56*

a

READING COMPREHENSION   *Page 56*

2. f	4. e	6. c
3. d	5. a	

BUILD YOUR VOCABULARY   *Page 56*

2. hospital   6. teddy bear
3. millionaire   7. boss
4. stocks   8. rich
5. earn

STORY 2   DRESSING FOR SUCCESS

Before You Read   *Page 58*

2. job interview, party   6. home
3. party, home   7. home
4. job interview, party   8. home
5. party, home   9. job interview, party
Note: Other answers may be possible.

Reading Skills

BUILD YOUR VOCABULARY   *Page 60*

2. b   4. a   6. b
3. a   5. b

READING COMPREHENSION   *Page 61*

2. T   7. F (Working women donate the clothes.)
3. F (didn't pay)   8. T
4. T   9. T
5. T   10. T
6. T

REVIEW THE VOCABULARY   *Page 62*

2. donate   5. interview
3. support   6. owner
4. confident

Put It Together

LET'S REVIEW   *Page 62*

2. stocks   4. family   6. married
3. store   5. friend   7. suit

Unit 6   Lifestyles

STORY 1   A YEAR WITHOUT TV

Before You Read

A.   *Page 66*

1. People: mother, parents, boy, father
2. Entertainment: TV, computer games, cards, reading
3. Time: year, evening, day, night
4. Feelings: happy, love, like, bored

Reading Skills

READING COMPREHENSION   *Page 68*

2. c	4. d	6. f
3. e	5. a	7. b

SENTENCE STUDY   *Page 68*

2. c	4. e	6. f
3. d	5. a	

STORY 2   BUY NOTHING DAY

Before You Read   *Page 70*

B. Use current calendar to complete this section.

Reading Skills

READING COMPREHENSION   *Page 71*

2. ads telling us to "buy, buy, buy"
3. Vancouver, British Columbia
4. read stories, sang songs, and painted pictures
5. We buy too much.
6. to tell people about Buy Nothing Day
7. Restaurants in the neighborhood donated the food.
8. not to buy anything November 29

BUILD YOUR VOCABULARY   *Page 72*

2. d	6. g
3. f	7. h
4. b	8. c
5. a	

REVIEW THE VOCABULARY   *Page 73*

3. place	8. person	13. thing
4. thing	9. thing	14. place
5. person	10. place	15. thing
6. place	11. person	16. place
7. holiday	12. holiday	

Put It Together

LET'S REVIEW   *Page 74*

2. Newspaper ads tell people to buy things before Christmas.
3. Every evening, Ryan Ruby played games or read the newspaper.
4. Students in New Mexico had a spaghetti dinner to tell people about Buy Nothing Day.
5. People in many countries celebrate Buy Nothing Day on November 29.
6. When the year was over, Ryan watched his favorite TV shows.

Unit 7   At Home

Let's Get Ready   *Page 77*

2. A	4. C	6. B
3. G	5. F	7. E

STORY 1 HOME, SWEET HOME

Before You Read   *Page 78*

A.

Things in the picture:
1, 2, 3, 4, 6, 8, 10

B.

2. sound   4. cakes
3. honey   5. sweet

Reading Skills

READING COMPREHENSION   *Page 80*

2. there was something in the wall
3. made a big hole in the wall
4. bees, a big beehive
5. hundreds
6. honey

READING COMPREHENSION   *Page 80*

4, 1, 3, 2, 5

BUILD YOUR VOCABULARY   *Page 81*

A.

2. honey   4. bees   6. relatives
3. walls   5. pail   7. tall

STORY 2 STUCK ON DUCT TAPE

Before You Read   *Page 82*

B.

1. tape, thumbtack   4. tape, staple
2. glue, tape, staple   5. glue, tape, staple
3. glue, tape   6. glue, tape
Note: Other answers may be possible.

Reading Skills

READ FOR THE MAIN IDEA   *Page 83*

c

REVIEW THE VOCABULARY *Page 84*

2. use
3. use
4. description
5. description
6. use
7. use

8. description
9. description
10. use
11. description
12. use

BUILD YOUR VOCABULARY *Page 84*

2. D
3. S

4. S
5. S

6. D

Put It Together

LET'S REVIEW *Page 85*

2. homes
3. holes
4. basement

5. tape
6. silver

7. wallet
8. duct

Unit 8   Seeing Double

Let's Get Ready *Page 87*

2. g
3. a

4. c
5. h

6. f
7. b

8. e

STORY 1   THE TWINS DAY FESTIVAL

Before You Read *Page 88*

A.
2. mother
3. sisters

4. identical
5. same

6. sound
7. wife

B.
1. F
2. T
3. T

4. T
5. T

Reading Skills

READING COMPREHENSION   *Page 90*

2. 2,500 to 3,000 sets of identical twins
3. babies, children, teenagers, and adults
4. meet old friends, make new friends, have competitions, eat hot dogs, play games, take pictures (any three)
5. love
6. Twins are very close. It's hard for a non-twin to understand this special relationship.
7. The non-twins feel lonely and left out. Many get divorced.
8. Doug, Phil, Jill, and Jena
9. "Will you marry me (us)?"

BUILD YOUR VOCABULARY   *Page 91*

2. a   4. b
3. b   5. b

STORY 2   TWO PLUS TWO

Before You Read   *Page 92*

2. carpenter, daycare worker
3. washing clothes, dusting furniture
4. T-shirts, jeans
5. TV, stereo

Reading Skills

READING COMPREHENSION *Page 94*

2. T	5. T	8. F Jill and Jena
3. F one TV	6. T	9. F in a daycare center
4. T	7. F are happy	10. T

BUILD YOUR VOCABULARY *Page 95*

2. happy	6. married
3. together	7. twin
4. morning	8. cooking
5. jeans	

REVIEW THE VOCABULARY *Page 95*

2. dust	6. clean
3. sleep	7. wear
4. look	8. live
5. cook	

Put It Together

LET'S REVIEW *Page 96*

A.

Across
   5. sisters
   8. identical
   9. wife
   10. Festival

Down
   1. together
   2. house
   3. two
   5. same
   6. twins
   7. clean

B. *Page 97*

2. different	5. new	8. smallest
3. non-twin	6. divorce	9. adults
4. sister	7. unlucky	10. single

Unit 9   Working Overtime

Let's Get Ready   *Page 99*

A.

2. f	5. b	8. c
3. e	6. d	9. h
4. j	7. i	10. a

> STORY 1   HELP ON WHEELS

Reading Skills

READING COMPREHENSION   *Page 101*

2. a	4. a	6. b
3. b	5. a	

BUILD YOUR VOCABULARY   *Page 102*

Group B: work   Group C: relax   Group D: customer

BUILD YOUR VOCABULARY   *Page 103*

A.

2. cold	6. people
3. women	7. husband
4. strong	8. repairs/fixes
5. job	

> STORY 2   THE SINGING DOCTOR

Before You Read   *Page 104*

2. doctor	5. doctor	8. singer
3. doctor	6. singer	9. doctor
4. singer	7. doctor	10. doctor

Reading Skills

READING COMPREHENSION   *Page 106*

2. b	6. a
3. b	7. a
4. a	8. b
5. b	

BUILD YOUR VOCABULARY   *Page 107*

A.

2. patients	6. sing
3. show	7. smile
4. songs	8. good
5. medical	

REVIEW THE VOCABULARY   *Page 107*

2. d	4. a
3. e	5. c

Put It Together

LET'S REVIEW   *Page 108*

2. doctor	5. accident	8. show
3. hospital	6. song	9. mechanic
4. road	7. smile	10. patient

Unit 10   Two Chewy Tales

Let's Get Ready   *Page 110*

2. F	4. E	6. C
3. A	5. B	

STORY 1   WATCH OUT FOR THE DOLL!

Reading Skills

READING COMPREHENSION   *Page 113*

2. ~~sister~~ mother
3. ~~laughed~~ screamed
4. ~~teacher~~ mother
5. ~~knife~~ scissors
6. ~~hand~~ head
7. ~~real~~ plastic

8. ~~easy~~ difficult
9. ~~birthday~~ Christmas
10. ~~Two~~ Five
11. ~~daycare center~~ store
12. ~~returned~~ kept

BUILD YOUR VOCABULARY   *Page 114*

2. b
3. a

4. b
5. b

6. a

UNDERSTAND THE PRONOUNS   *Page 115*

2. the teacher
3. Mrs. Kenton
4. the doll

5. the children's
6. the batteries
7. some people

STORY 2   A CHEWY SUBJECT

Before You Read   *Page 116*

A.
2. T
3. F

4. T
5. T

6. T

Reading Skills

UNDERSTAND THE DETAILS   *Page 118*

2. c
3. b

4. e
5. a

6. f
7. g

SCAN FOR THE DETAILS *Page 118*

2. teacher
3. Sweden
4. rubber
5. everyone in the U.S. phone books
6. Utah
7. They thought there was too much gum to clean up.
8. Put your gum here.
9. on the sign

BUILD YOUR VOCABULARY *Page 119*

A.

2. tooth	6. rubber
3. success	7. liquids
4. trash can	8. modern
5. phone book	

Put It Together

LET'S REVIEW *Page 120*

8 Things in the House	8 Places	8 Days, Dates, or Times
chair	Utah	Christmas
table	daycare center	every day
scissors	Sweden	1870
batteries	Mexico	9,000 years ago
phone book	school	the day after Christmas
table	United States	half an hour
trash can	Statue of Liberty	1892
plastic cups	store	today

ACKNOWLEDGMENTS (*continued*)

Used by permission of Howard Dill. "The Engine That Purred." Used by permission of Daniel McDowall and Sandro Ravazzano. "Alligator Attack!"Used by permission of Loretta E. Keith. "Dressing for Success." Used by permission of Pallas Hansen. "A Year without TV." Used by permission of Anne Ruby. "Home, Sweet Home." Used by permission of Loren and Mary Van Sinclair. "Two Plus Two." Used by permission of Jean and Phil Malm and Jill and Doug Malm. "Help on Wheels." Used by permission of Jenny Woznuk. "The Singing Doctor." Used by permission of Dr. Nick Petrella. "A Chewy Subject." Adapted from "A Sticky Subject" by Roy Rivenburg from the *Los Angeles Times,* September 19, 1993, as condensed in *Reader's Digest*, February 1996.